LETTER TO EARTH

Letter to Earth

ELIA WISE

INSPIRED COMPANY

Published by INSPIRED COMPANY
P.O. Box 10
Mill Valley, California 94942

Wise, Elia
Letter to earth/ Elia Wise

Library of Congress Cataloging Card Number
97-090695

ISBN 0-9625678-1-7

Printed in the United States of America

First edition
1 3 5 7 9 10 8 6 4 2

We must expand our imaginations to include the truth.

My beloved daughter,

From the time I was old enough to grasp that life is an every day event, I wanted to know how it all works, who we all are and why we are here. Most people ask these questions in one way or another. Some devote their lives to mapping the seas of discovery. And a rare, well-charted few, aligned with fortitude and unfathomable grace, actually drop anchor at the shores of promised land. I, your mother, who counts the raisins that go into your cereal each morning, am one of these.

I do not live a saintly life and my experience is unlike any model of transcendence or enlightenment that spiritual history or popular culture has yet offered. I am a lover rather than a minister of love; an originator rather than a devotee; a doer rather than a meditator; and a straight-talker, who stirs up the stuck stuff on the bottom of the pot, rather than a harmonizer. I aspire to equal myself rather than humble myself to that source we have called God—the challenge is humbling enough. My greatest strengths are courage, discernment and devotion. My shortsuits are too many to list and apparently irrelevant to the nonjudgmental Universe that has opened to me its gates of knowledge.

While I have made every effort to clearly explain that I am a *person* who has expanded into the Universal dimensions of reality, for the rest of your life you may have to explain that you are not an E.T. and that your mother did not say she was an E.T. either. I do not know what else you may have to grapple with as a result of these writings. It is my hope that our brothers and sisters upon this struggling Earth will rise above their impulse to polarize, discredit or sensationalize, and will receive this book with open heart and mind. The time is so right. The need is so great.

Perhaps by the time you are old enough to read and digest what I have offered here, the world will be directing itself toward integrity, love and participation in the Greater Universe. In my time it is not yet so. While we seem to be gaining recognition of ourselves as a civilization in need of personal enlightenment and social transformation, we are a humanity whose spiritual glue has dried up. Our unity is broken into little pieces that are here and there scattered, too brittle to be reused. While healing forces are emerging among a large transformational community, as of yet we have no apparent medium for sticking ourselves back together. Like Post-it notes, we adhere to hopes and prospects for true fulfillment until some brusque encounter dislodges our gentle cohesion and we find ourselves separated once again from anything larger to which we add meaning.

In this climate, spiritual searching, a desire for simplicity and a reverence for nature are redirecting the lives of many millions of people. There is no question to those of us who have already crossed the threshold, that humanity is in a process of transmutation as big as the leap from protozoa to cell.

In liberating ourselves from a mechanistic world view we are readying ourselves to experience a spirit-endowed Universe and the multidimensional nature of essential reality.

Once upon a time there was no Earth...and then there was.
Once upon a time there was no ocean life...and then there was.
Once upon a time there was no animal life...and then there was.
Once upon a time there was no human life...and then there was.
Once upon a time there was no energy life...and then there was.
Once upon a time there was no multidimensional life...
Once upon a time there was no Universal spirituality...

In an effort to make its way from the realms of gods, saints, prophets and gurus, into the experience of people's lives, enlightenment is struggling to reincarnate in a new collective conception. You and the children of your time have the opportunity to begin this incarnation of enlightenment.

If I could craft for you a code to live by, a handful of simple practices that will serve you steadfast when you feel lost or confused, it might be this: With love, compassion, trust and creativity...be honest and straightforward about what you want, need, and feel, and respect the integrity of these to your nature. Love the truth of a moment more than anything you might wish would be there. Try to see what lives in a moment before you put anything there. Discern your knowing voice from all other voices, streams of thought or desires. Experience values without judgment. And cultivate courage of action, so your vision and understanding can be expressed as your life.

You have told me that I am getting tattered and torn from love, like the *Velveteen Rabbit*. I can think of no better way to use myself up. I recommend it to you when it is your turn to use yourself up.

You are a great Being in a little body, my dear child—a jewel of being. It is effortless for you to create joy and harmony around you and to remind the rest of us of our essential nature. Where other children may have family, you have many adult friends who come to our home and lift you in their arms. These friends are the visionaries and way-makers of our global awakening. You do not know them as great thinkers and planetary healers important to transforming the world. You know them as important to you. They lift you because your fullness of spirit is irresistible to them…and in holding you, they touch the future to which their lives are devoted. They honor your purity and clarity in meeting the world, when you choose not to be where grown-ups or children push, compete or otherwise mistreat one another. They bow with respect when you show no interest in amassing or possessing things. They celebrate your innate sense of integrity when they read to you from Beatrix Potter and you cringe at the fox's pretense of being a friend to Jemima Puddle-duck. Even in the stages of early childhood that are thought to be troublesome you have been generous, full of humor and wise. These riches that are yours for the sharing are felt by all who meet you.

You cannot run home open-armed to share your songs and stories of the day with these friends who see you truly. They are neither family nor frequent visitors, but they are deeply connected to the fulfillment of your potential. They listen to you with consummate respect and leave you with lasting treasures of self worth and appreciation. As you grow older you will hear their names outside our home. You will read their ideas, discuss their contributions, and realize that your childhood was embraced by the same arms that held the transformative vision of humanity.

You are a child of the Universe, my beloved daughter. As you grow, she will be informing you of her wisdom...and by and by, you will become conscious of yourself as the whole of the Universe in formation. I have written this book so you will know what I have learned in that process. You will need this information when you become restless with the narrow questions and incomplete answers of worldly education.

You are only three years old now and I am fifty. One day, while you are still in the practice of growing, your curiosity will set you on a deer run. Fueled by an alchemical mix of love and pain, and by your Soul's desire for unity, you will seek the unseen dimensions of yourself. There, in the reunion of self and Soul, when All That Is becomes all that is you, will you find the constant, pure and infinite love you are seeking. Then will its strands of intent be recognizable to you in every imperfect love the world offers you.

When I am too much your worldly mother to be listened to as mentor, or not there to guide you artfully through spirited inquiry and into multidimensional reality, you will have these writings to grow from and to celebrate as your lineage. Explore these thoughts, my dear one. Inhabit their possibility until their reality becomes you...or, if you are feeling unsure, embrace what serves you and leave for another moment that which you do not yet understand.

Last evening at dinner, after much imaginative play directed at resolving your feelings about the slaughter of pigs and the death of Charlotte in *Charlotte's Web*, you delivered one of your profound insights about life and death. "I think we all come here to get the courage of life," you said, "and then we go back where we came from and make a big circle around everything."

When you had not yet turned three and we had just moved into our little "cabin" in the trees, you awoke in the middle of the night. I was working on this book in the next room and I heard your stirrings. I ended my work, came in and slipped into bed beside you. Moments later you sat straight up, looked out the skylight into the glorious moonlit night and said to me, "Mama, the dark is sliding off the moon."

It is, my beloved. Indeed it is.

Thank you for the joy and comfort you bring to my life.

I love you eternally,

Mama

Dear People of Earth,

I know many of you are struggling with the pains and conflicts brought about by greed, inequality and personal disappointment. I know you are frightened by the isolation you feel, the apparent inadequacies of human nature, and the violence and sickness in your lives. I know most of you are preoccupied with the mainten-ance of survival, while only a handful of you have found your way to abundance. I know it weighs heavily on you that so many of those who have found abundance have done so with little concern for others. I know too few relationships work, too many people are injured by destructive childhood experiences, too few people feel truly loved, and too few dreams of a better future are believed in —but you do not know what to do to change it.

I have lived my whole life with you in these struggles. I fell to Earth from between my mother's legs, as all Earth babies do—but my search has carried me beyond human origin, into multidimensional experience and the source of my Being. This journey of multidimen-sional awakening is not exclusive. It is available to you as it was to me. We are all indigenous peoples of the Universe. In transcending the assumed boundaries of our local identity, each of us moves toward unification with our own Soul identity. Since the Soul is multidimensional in nature, it follows naturally that in expanding beyond our local identity each of us comes into reunion with dimensions of ourself that are nonlocal. In this way we are all extraterrestrials. We are all participants in the Greater Universe.

In my reunion of local, temporal self with multidimensional and eternal Soul, a merging occurred that informed me of the cumulative experience and understanding of all human manifestations my Soul has ever expressed. I was so transformed by this spiritual amalgamation that my former worldly identity dissolved into the background of a newfound multidimensional selfhood.

After this Soul unification I experienced the recapitulation of all Creation. In collective with numerous other Souls, I experienced moving from energy into substantive form to create the Earth herself. Then, individuating once again, we manifest ourselves as Earth's elements and components—her trees, water, gases, sea life, animal life, mineral life, and all that is integral to the nature of the Earth. I experienced this transfiguration and I studied the process by it which was done.

In all of this I was graced with insight and love of a magnitude that a self cannot contain without expansion into Soulhood and its enlightenment.

My seeking began with great sincerity when I was eight years old. When I was twenty-two I was met by a Being of extraordinary nature. She told me she had been born on the Earth, but was not from the Earth. Given her ability to manifest what common reality calls impossible, I believed her. For four years I gave myself to her tutelage, allowing her to show me the Universe as she knew it. Her stewardship of my exploration of the Universe was naturally mind altering and ultimately transformative. Having given her blanket permission, she popped me in and out of other dimensions of reality at her will. Like Arthur with Merlin, when I wanted to know what it was like to be an old growth tree, she propelled me into another state and I became a tree. The transitional process in these experiences was so fast and fluid it took twelve years of trying before I could track it and articulate its nature.

Not being the verbal type, my mentor did very little explaining of the nature of things and said almost nothing about our process together—although I tried continually to illicit spoken guidance and wisdom. Her way of teaching was to enable my direct experience. She told me that explaining it was my job.

I still cannot fully comprehend this Being, in her abilities or her inconsistencies. But I can attribute all the phenomena I experienced with her to one splendid capacity: her ability to dissolve the seeming separations between things.

There are many such Beings in the world, coming from different planetary and dimensional realities on various types of missions. To bring their Universal knowledge into the context of our understanding, several Universal Beings have been born here. There is no better way to bring something to life than to *be* it.

In the process of stalking the wild truth of my spirituality and human potential, I have come to know myself as one of these Beings. Remembering myself as a Universal Being and integrating this multidimensional nature with my human identity took several years of purposeful work. Since that integration occurred, the resulting combinant consciousness has enabled me to serve as a communicator, educator and translator between humanity and the Greater Universe. My heart and mind are equally aligned with both.

Acknowledging such a role publicly is fraught with challenges. We live in a time that is profoundly supportive of seeking. Whether it be seeking of health, spirituality or sustainability, everywhere people are seeking. Yet we have no contemporary models and little tolerance for *finding*. Those who claim to have found answers can be perceived as threatening—as if their gained strength implies a weakness in others, or could impose reality or prescribe behavior for others. When I meet this resistance I try to embrace it as the immune system of the dying body of thought and the dying body politic, fighting for survival. The human collective still needs this resistance; it controls our pace of transformation. If we make changes before there is a new convergence of vision and action, our collective body may die in the chaos before it accomplishes transformation. We do not want death. We want transformative healing.

Because I understand far more than I know how to *be*, I have been reluctant to publicly offer my insight into the nature of our Universe, concerned that it might be an act of spiritual hubris or arrogance. Although I experience the purity of my devotion and intent, it confounds me that the Universe has overlooked my shortcomings and graced me with multidimensional experience as an integral part of my daily life. I accept this as a demonstration of the unconditional love that embraces our humanness. It is because my heart aches for all of us, and for the condition of our world, that I now feel compelled to offer what measure of wisdom I may have.

The understanding shared in this book comes from traveling through and beyond control and fear, into realms of energetic and spiritual reality that brought me to reunion with my Soul and the nature of the Universe. The insight and vantage point I share may seem extraordinary, but they are not. I am only an early arrival at this convergence of self and Soul—an advance scout. Being so, I am charged with the challenge and the oppor-tunity of conveying the view and informing you of the nature of things. If I think of myself as the girl and young woman I was before I awakened, I could not even begin to write a book such as this. The presumption would be preposterous. And so I write this book to you from my Universal identity, from the wisdom I have gained in claiming my spirituality and my multidimensional origins.

I spent many months trying to write this book from the human point of view, identifying myself with the life we share on Earth. It was impossible for me to accomplish this book from that con-sciousness. I had to move into expanded dimensions of myself to perceive and articulate the workings of the Universe. It is because of this, rather than from any sense of superiority or separateness, that I speak of "you" on the Earth instead of "we" on the Earth. Forgive me this perch. Without it I do not know how to convey the view.

Previously unrecognized dimensions of reality are becoming self-evident to many upon the Earth at this time. The impact is sufficient to stimulate a shift that will redefine human values and priorities, transforming worldly reality. Such change is not without upheaval, intensified polarity between old and new, deep personal challenges of innovation and transformation, and false prophets. I encourage you to question any Being who represents greater consciousness without demonstrating it as love. I caution you not to confuse your understanding of the ideas and knowledge coming forth at this time, with genuine expansion of your beingness. Ideas and knowledge alone do not expand Beings. Love is the expander. Without it we will have little more than a new information age. With it, humanity will enter the time of its realization—an Age of Inspired Realism.

As Earth is very close to a time of intensified interaction with the Greater Universe, the people of Earth and those who populate the Cosmos need to correspond experience, information and understanding. I am writing this book to open such a dialogue, to stimulate your inner knowing, and to help you attune to an informed and heartful state of inquiry that can bring you into your own multidimensionality and direct knowledge of the Universe.

You will, no doubt, have questions or insights beyond those I have addressed in the pages that follow. At the back of this book you will find letter paper for correspondence between us. Please write back. We are here to illuminate one another. As a spokesperson for a collective of Universal Beings, I will answer as many questions as I am able, through as many forms of communication as become available during the unfolding of this dialogue.

I invite you to join me on a journey into the Universe.
It is the ultimate in adventure travel.

In Love,

∾ LETTERS TO EARTH ∾

How do we in the Cosmos
know when you need our help?
Do we hear you?

*W*E DO "HEAR" YOU. If you follow an inquiry or exploration to its furthest point in the available resources of your planet and are still unable to fulfill your pursuit, you will initiate a stimulus into the Universe. *Until* you have exhausted your local resources, however, your stimulus is in play in the world as if it were the ball in a racket ball game. It continues to bounce off all available walls and angles until it comes back to you with what you need, or until it delivers what you need from a series of plays. If what you are seeking is *beyond* the limits of the court, you get to bounce it off the Universe.

You do not have to send a call into the Cosmos intentionally. It happens anyway. It is the nature of inquiry to stimulate response. Any Being in the Universe can stimulate a response from any or all others. In this way all knowledge, wisdom and love in the Universe is available to you.

If you are seeking answers, you need to ask questions and be available to receive a response—wherever it may come from. It could come from the grocer, the radio, the garden or the Cosmos.

If you diffuse the focus of an inquiry with many simultaneous inquiries, you may succeed in transmitting several or all of them. It is unlikely, however, that you will know which feedback is coming into your life in response to which inquiry. If you abandon an inquiry or diffuse its focus with impatience, anger or confusion, your stimulus can lose its broadcast clarity. When this happens your question or need does not transmit to us discernibly. You are most effective when you focus on one discovery at a time and allow the response to unfold.

Simple quietude and focus will maximize your broadcast and reception clarity. This is why meditative, contemplative and dream states provide such fertile ground for dialogue with the Universe. When you become well practiced at internal quietude and focus, you will be able to maintain conscious interaction with the Universe even while you are engaged in the noise and activity of the world.

It takes much less time for your stimulus to reach us than it does for our response to reach you—if our response conforms to the time and space of your reality. It takes time for the Universe to inform you through practical experience. It takes no time at all for the Universe to inform you through your contemplative, meditative or feeling experience—if you are ready for the discovery. Getting ready, however, can take years.

When your stimulus moves through the Universe it is not a general call for assistance from any Being who happens to be free at the moment. The stimulus you send is specific to the essence of your inquiry. Only a Being who embodies the full realization of what you are seeking will be impacted by your call.

Each Being in the Universe embodies and expresses a unique frequency. These frequencies are not handed out like social security numbers; they come to life when we do. They are us. For each of us in the Universe, our frequency is our first, most essential and eternal identity. To be a unique frequency is to have a unique value. Each Being in the Universe has a unique value—in both the mathematical and conceptual sense. There is no duplication. Each frequency/value has the capacity to manifest in infinite ways. Since Human Beings are also Universe Beings, you share these origins of frequency and value. This means that you have the capacity to manifest in infinite ways.

While you are individuated by your own unique frequency/value, you are also a component within larger collectives of frequencies and values. Humanity often refers to its collectivity as the *collective unconscious* or the *collective consciousness*. In fact, each individual identity on Earth is a component of numerous collective identities. You are a component of your Soul collective, your ethnic collective, your gender collective, your species collective, your planetary collective and, ultimately, the Universal collective.

The simultaneity of your individuality and your collectivity is just one demonstration of the capacity of Human Beings to express themselves in numerous states concurrently. As children of the Universe you are by nature multidimensional Beings, even when your awareness is focused in the three spatial dimensions and one time dimension currently known to Earth.

All Beings and life forms in the Universe are able to interact with each other—no matter how many dimensions we are focused in, no matter what state of being we inhabit and no matter where we are in time and/or space. What makes this possible? Every Being in the Universe embodies every frequency in the Universe. This provides each Being with an inherent intercom for communicating with all other Beings. While the whole is embodied in each of us, each Being has a different frequency/value that is central to its beingness. In the Greater Universe we call the frequency/value that is uniquely central to each of us our axial value. The axial value of each Being governs its stimuli, responses, magnetism and coherence. Since no two Beings have the same value as their axis, no two Beings configure the Universe in the same way. The axial value of each Being organizes all other frequencies relative to itself. As a result, each one of us is the Universe, constellated in a unique way.

Each Being's *axial value* lives as a supporting value within all other Beings. This means my integrity and self-realization intrinsically informs and supports yours, and your integrity and self-realization intrinsically informs and supports mine. This is the relationship of each of us to all others, regardless of our state of being or location in the Universe. The trees, the stars, the mineral kingdom and non-local Beings can communicate with you because they are already within you as an integral part of your Being. All of us are empowered in this way.

Your axial value travels with you *as* you. Everywhere you go you constellate that value. You are its tuning fork, its artist, its agent, its advocate, its champion. You are not aware that you are taking a particular value with you everywhere you go because you have never been any place it was not. What enters a room when you do? What diminishes when you are gone? You might be the last to know the value that makes you, *you*. Others sense it, but they can rarely name it. It tunes them up when you arrive and it recedes within them—or reintegrates with increased amplitude—when you depart.

Those of us who are facilitators of interdimensional communication have the opportunity to go anywhere in the Universe that our frequency, or axial value, is called for to fortify or catalyze consciousness. The Cosmic/Earth feedback loop depends entirely upon stimulus and response ability.

There are as many ways to answer a call as there are needs. On this occasion I have chosen to answer my call by being born on the Earth as a Human Being, to bring my consciousness here in a package called my *self*. This is a highly impractical approach for most Universal Beings and most purposes. A lifetime seems to take so long once you are living it—and one has to be there the whole time. In answering *this* call, however, it is the perfect means for bringing my frequency and value to life on Earth.

Whether a single individual or a collective reaches us with a stimulus, we respond to the call spontaneously—just as you do when your telephone rings. Usually you do not know who is calling or what they are calling about. As Universal Beings dedicated to interdimensional self-realization, we know we are being called upon to provide the unique frequency we embody to someone, somewhere, who is aspiring to realize that value. To accomplish this we merge our consciousness with the consciousness of the person transmitting the stimulus. If you are the one sending the call, the Universal Being who embodies what you are seeking merges with your consciousness. Once this merge has occurred, you will find that you have access to greater levels of understanding and to pathways of thought that further your course of discovery. Since the idea of Human consciousness has been introduced, it is best to define it.

Human consciousness is the capacity to focus, direct and make meaningful the self-awareness of being.

Our merge with you does not enlighten you. We do not *give* you consciousness. Rather, we respond to your stimulus by making available to you avenues of understanding which are not readily accessible to you in your local reality system. Through such relationships of stimulus and response, all states of being and all planets and dimensions have equal access to the whole of Universal consciousness. *Whether* you use Universal resources and *how* you use them is entirely up to you.

How do you know if a Universal Being is helping you? Without apparent explanation you find you have gained clarity, insight or inspiration that you did not have previously. You inexplicably rise above the emotionality, complexity or invisibility of an issue, gaining a more mature overview. This is a frequent demonstration of cosmic assistance. More dramatically and less often, Universal help will engage you internally in a momentary alteration of reality. Because this kind of experience informs you subjectively, it is usually difficult to validate, duplicate or communicate to others. You can gain inspiration or insight by reflecting on the experience, but the alchemy lives in the moment of its happening.

In instances where our response to your inquiry is best provided through life experience, we merge our consciousness with yours so that you may perceive your experiences from a fresh perspective. A merge can briefly liberate your rhythms and frequency patterns to allow an enlightening alteration of reality: you will see new things or perceive old things in a new way. In these instances our merge optimizes your experience. A merge can also temporarily boost the qualitative intensity of your focus. When this happens the magnetism of your personal energy field is intensified, affecting the quality of what you draw to yourself and the speed at which you attract it. In this way our merge helps you to produce experience.

When these breakthroughs occur the Universe Being you are communing with may be your own Soul, who holds the accumulated wisdom of all experience in which you have ever participated. When you are feeling overwhelmed or inadequate however, you tend to think you need help from something *greater than yourself*, rather than from *your greater self*. More often than not your answer or guidance will come from your own knowing self—your Soul. When you do not believe in your knowing self, or when the frequency you are seeking cannot be effectively communicated from your knowing self, the Universe Being who can best catalyze your discovery is the one who merges with you.

In most instances we do not need to identify your exact location in time and space in order to respond to your stimulus. Without pause we just allow our consciousness to be magnetized wherever it is needed. In this way we effortlessly assist other Beings in realizing within themselves the values that we embody. Since we know ourselves to have integrity everywhere in the Universe we do not have to know where we are going in order to feel secure. This is a great advantage of Universal consciousness.

Only occasionally do we who support you from the Cosmos know the content of our merge with you. Our experience is more often energetic than cognitive. Frequently we deduce the content of a merge in which we have participated by observing a change that seems to have our signature on it. This has probably happened to you. Imagine finding yourself preoccupied for a few weeks with thoughts about interactive computer programs that could help people learn empathy. This is a highly specific and unexplainable random theme. Months later your local news reports on a newly developed computer program designed to develop empathy. "How amazing," "How ironic," or "How curious," you might think. Unless you understand the workings of the Universe, it is unlikely you would think, "I helped work that idea through," "I responded as part of a random sample," or "I picked this up on cosmic news while it was in development." But you *did*!

Those of us who express ourselves by building bridges of interplanetary and interdimensional communication are always looking for opportunities to integrate our consciousness into new dimensions. It serves us, it serves you and it serves the conscious unification of the Universe.

No two Beings ever come together for the benefit of only one.

The stimulus/response relationship between us is a two-way street. Often we in the Greater Universe seek understanding that only you on Earth can provide. In these cases we are the stimulus and you are the response. I am drawn to Earth as much for the fulfillment of my dreams as for yours. It is my dream to see the understanding that I embody—my frequency/value—expressed throughout the Universe. Humanity dreams of living in a world where the value of each person is recognized and appreciated, and Humanity dreams of understanding the nature of the Universe. Your dreams invite me here to make my dream come true.

Who runs the switchboard?
Is there a God?

*T*HE STUFF OF WHICH EVERYTHING in the Universe is made is *energy, life force,* or *chi.* Energy is like alphabet soup—all the letters needed to make any word are in the soup, but some conscious force has to select and organize them for words, sentences and paragraphs to come into being. Like a word created from the soup, the unique frequency/value that each one of us embodies is a constellation of energy created by a conscious stimulus.

───────────── ⌣⌣ ─────────────

There is no grand puppeteer moving you around by invisible strings. The creative Source endows all energy with the self-governing power of integral intelligence. Every value in the Universe is interactive and interdependent in one integrated circuit. So well is the Universe endowed that all beingness, down to the smallest microparticle, possesses the intelligence of the whole. This intelligence is not necessarily cognitive. It is an essential vibrational and magnetic intelligence inherent to all energy.

───────────── ⌣⌣ ─────────────

There are dimensions beyond the three spatial dimensions and one time dimension currently perceived on Earth, in which the language of all consciousness, of all beingness, is the same. This is the language of *stimuli*. In three dimensional realities these stimuli are experienced as *vibrations*. Vibrations are the local broadcast signal of each frequency/value. In the dimension of essential stimuli, all frequencies/values can manifest the full spectrum of their potential. This dimension of being is the switchboard, or the *where*, of the integrated circuit. The stimuli broadcast within this dimension generate responses in the reality systems to which they have relevance. Any sense of fate or predestination derives from this relationship between the Universal stimuli and the Earthly responses of your own frequency/value.

All states and forms of being throughout the Universe are in constant and spontaneous communication with one another through their essential stimuli and response ability.

Vibrations convey themselves as energetic presences and are usually identified by the way they are felt. You know this experience when you enter a room full of people and feel the "vibes." Vibrations also have visual, auditory and kinetic manifestations. With greater refinement of your subtle senses you can learn to perceive these manifestations.

The common source of all energy is the *who* you are looking for. We call this source "All That Is." Calling this source God and attributing infinite love, integrity, creativity and transformational capacity to God, reflects clear understanding of the source of all known realities. Attributing to God characteristics of dualism—good/bad, right/wrong, perfection/imperfection, master/supplicant, reward/punishment, obedient/disobedient—is misunderstanding. This misunderstanding furthers Human separation from the integrity of its origin. While such dualistic conditions do have reality in the world, they are the *inverted expressions* of essential values rather than being essential values themselves, and have no reality in the enlightened Universe.

The inherent attribute that enables any unit of energy to communicate with any other unit of energy is magnetism. *All energy, no matter how simple or complex and regardless of its location in the Universe, has the inherent capacity for magnetic interaction with all other energy. This magnetism is best described as* Sympathetic Vibrational Magnetism, (SVM). *This is not magnetism as the term is used specific to electromagnetism. Electromagnetism is just one discerned aspect of Universal magnetism. Sympathetic Vibrational Magnetism is fundamental to the nature of All That Is.*

To understand *Sympathetic Vibrational Magnetism* you need not be a scientist or a Cosmic Being. You need only be an attentive observer. You experience it every day, although you may not recognize it or name it. You think to call a particular friend and the phone rings, with your thought of friend calling you. The right book shows up at just the right moment. A word you have just learned seems to show up everywhere. A dream, a conversation or a passage read in childhood, emerges from memory twenty years later when its meaning is immediately relevant to your experience. The capacity for this magnetic interaction is inherent to all energy. It is *Sympathetic Vibrational Magnetism*.

In the past your civilization might have attributed such occurrences to an abstract psychic force, a sixth sense, serendipity or coincidence. Carl Jung observed this reoccurring phenomenon in Human experience and called it *synchronicity*. He defined synchronicity as "the meaningful coincidence of two or more events, where something other than the probability of chance is involved." *Sympathetic Vibrational Magnetism* is the "something other" to which Carl Jung refers. It is not only life and experience on Earth that are facilitated by *SVM*. All dimensions of the Universe coincide.

Occurrences of coincidence are not unexplainable phenomena. They are demonstrations of Sympathetic Vibrational Magnetism: the inherent capacity of a unit of energy to attract unto itself what it requires for its transformation or realization.

Picture an atom that has a free electron in its outer shell, searching for another atom that is lacking an electron in its outer shell. They have a yearning, something drawing them to find one another. The something is *Sympathetic Vibrational Magnetism*. Their chemical covalences exist as a medium for *SVM*. Chemical bonding is the result, or fulfillment, of their yearning. When the atoms come together there is realization. Each is transformed and something new is created. What is true for atoms is also true for larger constellations of energy. Whether yearning for wholeness or for temporary fulfillments, people are regularly drawn to one another and to opportunities that stimulate their transformation or self-realization.

To explore a few of the myriad ways *Sympathetic Vibrational Magnetism* enables reality to manifest, think of a cherry pie in the making. The crust is prepared. Cherries fresh-picked from the tree are being pitted to fill the shell. Until there are enough cherries to fill the shell, the cherry pie cannot fulfill its potential. If the baker runs out of cherries he will not use whatever energy may be at hand—oranges, a pile of napkins, or the daily newspaper—to fill the remaining space in the pie shell. Rather, he will go after more cherry energy. In this example, *Sympathetic Vibrational Magnetism* calls for energy, or frequency, of like kind.

A cherry pie has a recipe and a baker who is in charge. It is easy to see who is the creator of the magnetism. In most of your life, however, it is not so obvious who is putting the ingredients of your life together. Sometimes it appears the cherries have jumped into the pie shell before measuring themselves, and to cover their tracks they have pulled in the daily newspaper. In fact, your whole life is something you are constantly cooking up. You are the baker, the magnetizer. All ingredients for all recipes are drawn from the Universe—from free energy or the energy constellated as your fellow Beings. While your magnetism is as specific as your need, you do not have to know which ingredients to put together to get what you need. Your part in the process is to provide a focused stimulus through feeling, intention or action, and to maintain an openness in your life to receive the response.

If you are a gourmet baker a flat of day-old cherries may not meet your standards. Depending on the discernment of your intention, *SVM* might narrow the selection pool to cherries in general or to the specific size, quality and variety needed to realize your intended pie. If the desired energy is not available to fulfill *SVM*—if the pie cannot be finished within the tolerances acceptable for the intended cherry pie—it is possible that nothing would be provided to finish the pie. As the baker, you could be called upon to redefine your intention in order to remain integral with the availabilities of the Universe. The cherry pie might be reconceived and transformed into cherry popovers, cherry tarts, compost or a lesson in planning. In this example *Sympathetic Vibrational Magnetism* demonstrates as a catalyst for change, producing what is needed for fulfillment by inspiring the baker to reconceive the intention. Where a resistant baker feels thwarted and even oppressed, a receptive baker lets go of the idea of pie or invents a new path to pie, experiencing creative challenge instead of limitation.

Consider yet another possibility within the myriad possibilities of *SVM*. When additional cherries cannot be found to complete the pie, if the baker opens the intention to invention, another resource can be magnetized. The only requirement of *SVM* is that whatever is magnetized resonates and cooperates successfully with the cherries. Cherry-orange, cherry-lemon or cherry-grape, could fail to be compatible. Without a catalyst or a harmonizing agent, their values might not integrate well and the pies would taste terrible. However, cherry and rhubarb could align to produce a pleasing taste sensation. In this example *Sympathetic Vibrational Magnetism* demonstrates as harmonious energy.

The Universe is designed to explore and fulfill its potential by facilitating transformation or facilitating realization.

Transformation is an idea that is easily understood. Water changes to steam or ice, anger turns to compassion, chrysalis metamorphoses to butterfly and yesterday becomes today. These are transformations that are accepted and understood. *Realization* of a Human Being, or of Humanity as a whole, is a less familiar idea. It is the making real of what is possible, bringing the potential of an individual or collective identity into actuality. Within this grand notion of realization each individual is having daily realizations, moments of understanding and moments of feeling that are little universes of enlightenment unto themselves.

All demonstrations of transformation and realization are the result of *Sympathetic Vibrational Magnetism*—energy attracting what is needed to realize the potential of the moment. Without this inherent magnetic intelligence of all energy, eggs and flour could not mix to become a cake, science would have no reoccurring patterns to test and measure, and you and I could not lend ourselves to each other in everchanging ways to help one another realize a project or a moment of meaningful experience.

Every time you initiate a course of action, creation, inquiry or feeling, you send a vibrational stimulus into the world. This vibrational broadcast operates like a "call for papers" or an employment advertisement. Instead of using the newspaper or mail solicitation, the medium is consciousness and the messenger is Sympathetic Vibrational Magnetism. Your stimulus is a magnetic call that ripples through the energy of the world—and possibly the Universe—scanning for resonance and seeking sympathetic alignments. As your stimulus magnetizes energy that is available for alignment or energy in like pursuit, the people, things, experiences, thought forms and feelings that embody this energy are drawn into your awareness. Some stimuli require years to magnetize the energy for their fulfillment or transformation. Some fulfill almost instantly. Your axial value and its amplitude govern your stimuli and responses, your coherence, and your magnetism.

~~~

Sympathetic Vibrational Magnetism enables responses to stimuli generated by your Being and intention, and it enables the stimuli of other Beings to elicit your responses. It is an interactive and co-creative dynamic of consciousness. From most vantage points in the Universe it is difficult to know whether you are the stimulus, the response or a contributing editor in any demonstration of *SVM*. And from most vantage points in the Universe it is irrelevant.

Energy is neither bad nor good. It just is. If you want to create a depression, an impression or an expression, you can attract what you need to fulfill your intention. This is true whether your intention is subconscious, conscious or superconscious. You can create suffering, joy, confusion or awe from the same source material. There is nothing judging or determining what you may create in the world. If there is a response to your stimulus, or if you respond to another's stimulus, realization of your intention is underway. If insufficient energy is magnetized to an intention of *local* relevance, you will find yourself in the position of the baker who is called upon to reconceive or transform his intention. If insufficient energy is magnetized and your intention is one of *Universal* relevance, your stimulus will extend into the Cosmos to find its response.

Your condition of integrity is constantly changing as you progress with intention, or mature by benefit of age and experience, toward the actualization of your potential. Your perception and understanding expand in such a way that aspects of reality formerly beyond your comprehension are magnetized into self-evidence by your readiness for their inclusion in your consciousness. The attribute of energy that enables you to draw forth what is needed in order to progress toward self-realization is Sympathetic Vibrational Magnetism.

The local and Universal stimuli being transmitted to your consciousness cover a vast spectrum of frequencies, as vast as All That Is. The ones you are likely to recognize and/or respond to fall within a relatively narrow band of the total spectrum. As you expand your response ability toward an all-inclusive state of integrity, you become instinctively, intuitively and cognitively interactive with a fuller spectrum of Universal stimuli. Those aspects of the total spectrum of reality which constellate at each newly achieved reception level become self-evident. Ideas and understandings already in existence are received and comprehended as if they were immediate and new.

This capacity of consciousness to magnetize from the total spectrum of existence exactly what is needed for a potential to become actual, is profound. Where does it stop? At the level of creating one's own reality? At the subatomic level? At a boundary between animate and inanimate objects? No. It is not finite. It permeates and integrates All That Is.

It could be argued that a book to which you are attracted at just the right moment has no identity consciousness of its own through which to cooperate in an *SVM* relationship.

Sympathetic Vibrational Magnetism does not require a self-conscious identity through which to operate. The frequency spectrum of any creation is a crystallized reflection of its creator at the time of its articulation. Each book maintains the vibrational state of its writer at the time of writing. Each recorded song maintains the vibrational states of its writer, singer, musicians and engineer. By this principle, all works of art and contributions to reality are equally capable of transmitting stimuli to your consciousness or providing responses to stimuli within your consciousness.

If you are willing to be an animist and bring all things to life, every tree, every book, every feeling, becomes a part of your dialogue with the Universe. A tree is not just a tree. Like your telephone lines, its branches reach out to connect life forces throughout the planet. A book on your shelf is not just a book. The person who wrote it is living in your house and contributing a frequency to your environment.

Is Humanity prepared to entertain the multidimensional significance of this inherent organizing and unifying principle within all nature? If you are ready to embrace the challenge, science will rapidly unify with the spiritual and metaphysical thinking previously relegated to philosophy or religion. Is this approaching unification not in itself a demonstration of *Sympathetic Vibrational Magnetism* and the capacity of all values to manifest their collective integrity?

Humanity is about to enter an *Age of Inspired Realism* in which Human intelligence unifies science with spirit, and creator with creation. In this age Humanity will grow to realize that there is only one nature. The fact that you have not yet built the bridges between linear and nonlinear realities, or between the visible and invisible, reflects unclaimed knowledge rather than impossibility.

As your comprehension of Universal nature increases you are likely to document the objective processes that correspond to all phenomenal occurrences. Ironically, the first stimulus or original creative resource may remain the one unprovable phenomenon. Perhaps it is only by implication, induction, appreciation and direct experience of the exquisite magnitude and purposeful order of our Universe, that any of us ever comes to know the loving nature of All That Is.

How were we chosen
for this dialogue with Humanity?

WE WHO CARRY ON THIS DIALOGUE with you were not chosen to come to Earth by a board, or a commission, or a group of superiors. While we do have mentors and teachers, we do not have superiors. We are each our own authority. Just as it is obvious to you who among you is tall enough to reach the top shelf of your closet without a stepladder, our areas of mastery are so apparent that our appropriateness to any service is obvious to all.

The Universal Beings who best embody the frequencies/values that are being explored and developed on your beautiful planet are the ones who come to Earth to help you bring these potentials to realization. These Beings do not actually have to *do* anything for the job to get done. Since they are the realization being sought, they simply have to *be*. They embody the answer and demonstrate it without device. The same way a tuning fork helps you find the note you want by ringing out its vibration, a Universal Being rings out an enlightened vibration so that you can match its value within yourself and bring it forth into personal expression. The very presence of this Being in your system of reality will serve to attune your consciousness to the value the Being embodies.

When Humanity is exploring any Universal value, the best assistance the Universe can provide is to send to Earth the Cosmic Being who embodies that axial value. Through that Being's self-integration into Earth life, the axial value the Being embodies becomes integrated into Human consciousness.

Whatever you integrate within your consciousness has your consciousness integrated within it. In this way, each measure of each Being's enlightenment moves the whole of the Universe towards unification.

Integralism is an example of a Universal value. When Humanity begins to explore the value of *integralism* a stimulus is transmitted into the Cosmos. The Universal Being who embodies the axial value of *integralism* has the opportunity to respond to your stimulus by coming to Earth. This can mean being born into a Human life. It can also mean making entry and participating through a medium that is more brief than a Human lifetime—flora, fauna, elemental condition.

Often, in its pursuit of self-knowledge, Humanity focuses on the exploration of a pivotal idea that is not a Universal value but derives from a Universal value. *Interdependence* is a Human idea stemming from a mechanistic perception of reality in which everything is part of a greater whole. The Universal value from which this idea derives is *integralism*, the holgraphic nature of reality wherein each aspect contains and is contained by the whole.

By coming to Earth in response to the derivative stimulus transmitted by Humanity's exploration of *interdependence*, the Universal Being who embodies the axial value of *integralism* can seed Human exploration of *interdependence* with the consciousness of *integralism*.

All the Universe is tied together by one life line. Enlightenment to *integralism* is eternally available to you through meditation, contemplation and revelation. You do not need a Universal Being to bring about its realization. The same contribution is made to the world by each person whose life becomes a demonstration of the essential value she or he embodies. This is self-realization. Once the enlightenment of any value is embodied on the Earth, what had been only internally and energetically available to you becomes an immediate, palpable and worldly stimulus for awakening your consciousness to that value. The Being who embodies the realization of a Universal value is like a solar generator for that value. You already have the sun, but a solar generator focuses and intensifies its power for practical applications.

Each of us has the capacity to illuminate a unique value of All That Is. When your life comes to express the realization of your value, enlightenment occurs. This has an omnipresent impact. The unobstructed consciousness of the essential value you embody beams forth its clarity throughout the Universe. What had been your light, strengthening as you grew, becomes a laser beam capable of permeating, informing and illuminating all Beings who are open to its gift. This is how you come to have eras or epochs of values, understanding and perception on Earth.

Do we who come
from beyond the Earth
actually live somewhere?

WHEN I DESCRIBE A COSMIC HOME that is within my experience you will appreciate why "There's no place like home." This home in the Cosmos is not a planet. It is a star that is currently invisible in your galaxy.

Everything in the Universe has form in some dimension, although it may not resemble form as you know it. Thought forms, light bodies and vibrational energy patterns are forms as real as your corporeal bodies. Form is defined by the system of reality in which a Being chooses to participate.

To manifest in any system of reality a Being must conform to that system's dimensional coordinates. When you are sailing in open waters with no land in sight, identifying coordinates of latitude and longitude locates you in relation to the invisible land and to the seemingly boundless sea. The same is true when you are navigating the multidimensional Universe. Dimensional coordinates, as well as coordinates of magnetism and frequency, locate you in relation to invisible systems of reality and seemingly boundless consciousness. Without these coordinates we would bump into each other more often than we do.

There are many Cosmic home bases among those of us who are born on Earth to serve as interdimensional communicators. I was born on the Earth as a Human Being in the 1940s. However, I also participate as a Universal Being in a reality system that is manifest both as a star in your galaxy and in dimensions people do not commonly recognize. This star is not known to Earth's astronomers because you cannot currently see it. It is where you think nothing is—in what appears to you to be a gap amidst other visible stars. Your scientists are trying to come to grips with this. They cannot explain the loss of mass at certain places in the Universe. They have named these places black holes in space. Scientists correctly understand a black hole in space to be a "place" where a star was once manifest. However, some believe the life of the star is over, having left behind a vacuum-like field.

A black hole in your dimensional space is another reality system whose coordinates interface with those of Earth. It is a locus of being for a collective identity, just as Earth is a locus of being for the collective Human identity. The collective or star referred to as a black hole is neither dead nor gone. Its focus of consciousness is just temporarily redirected into other dimensional coordinates that preclude its appearance in your space/time continuum. The field your scientists interpret to be unoccupiable and inescapable is actually holding the star's place in space, the way you might put a reserved sign on your airplane seat if you wanted to get off for a walk between legs of a flight. Because the collective identity of the star has taken a walk somewhere your consciousness cannot currently reach,

instead of perceiving its manifestation, you perceive it as
being sealed off behind its own event horizon—a gap in
your space/time continuum.

Imagine a photograph of a family all huddled together on the steps of their front porch, with the dog in the middle. Now imagine that someone has neatly cut out the image of the dog. When you look at the picture, in one sense you can still see the dog, because while its form is gone, it has left the exact outline of its image. This is what has happened with the identity that occupies a black or a white hole in space. Its form is temporarily located elsewhere, but nothing can occupy that space unless it fits the coordinates exactly, having total integrity with the established energy, form and function of that space.

The star where I participate as a Universal Being is populated by Beings who are integrally involved in supporting Earth's development. Our star is coordinated in the Universe in a way that enables each of us to manifest in any one of several different reality systems when the need arises. While we are free to travel anywhere in the Universe as consciousness *without* substantive form, our ability to manifest a substantive form is limited to those systems into which each of us has been born and lived a lifetime. Each life experience encodes us with the amplitudes of consciousness and the coordinates for manifestation that are necessary to locate ourselves with form in that system for purposeful visits.

This idea may sound like science fiction, but it could as easily describe the opportunities and limitations of your dream world.

You too are free to travel anywhere in the Universe as consciousness without substantive form. During sleep time and in other
altered states, you are able to awaken to other dimensions in which
you have lived. It seems that you get there without any effort. In
fact, it is impossible to get there at all without a pass-key for the
coordinates. Your access seems effortless because the coordinates
for entry are already encoded in your Being.

Until recently the star where I participate as a Universal Being
was a visible source of light in your galactic space. In recent years
however, our star has been beyond your visibility while our population retrains and readies itself to facilitate you in a collective
transmutation of consciousness. This transmutation will express
a change in the magnetism and frequency of the Earth and of all
that is born to her.

Our preparation for the privilege of assisting you in this process
required us to focus on our own individual and collective expansion. To exercise and study our own transmutability we precipi-
tated the growth of our collective into new dimensions of reality.
For this transmutation to be possible the consciousness of our
entire collective had to shift dimension by temporarily merging
into singularity. In that process, the coordinates of frequency and
magnetism needed to maintain our manifestation as a star within
your galaxy were surrendered. We became focused in aspects of
multidimensionality that are not yet within your awareness, causing
the visibility of our star to be temporarily absent from your galactic
space, leaving a reserved place—a black hole. You could say we
are shedding our light on different matter for a while.

Note: Our star will appear as either a black hole or a white hole in space, depending upon which dimensions you are in when observing it. From Earth's position our star would be perceived by astronomers as a black hole—a location where energy has reached singularity and "collapsed" inward. However if you were observing the Cosmos from the dimensions we have recently been born into through our collective transmutation, you would perceive our star as a white hole in space—a location where energy has reached singularity and expressed itself in an outward direction.

Removing ourselves from visibility in your galactic space did not remove us from interaction with you. We are actually more in touch with your intrapsychic dimensions of reality than we were previously, when our range of responsibility included the material aspects of your lives.

Both our presence in your galactic space and our temporary departure from it have everything to do with you. We are facilitating agents for the expansion of Humanity into multidimensionality and Universal consciousness. Until you entered your current transitional phase we served you where you were, supporting your efforts toward enlightenment, hoping to provide you with added impetus for growth. When you began accelerating into planetary readiness for transformation, we were stimulated to retreat to develop skills for facilitating the transmutation process that will enventuate from your transformational cycle.

Our recent collective expansion is analogous to your own forthcoming process. From our experience we are prepared to facilitate the internal equalizations and societal changes that will arise from your dimensional expansion. This does not mean we know what your planetary processes will look like. We do know that all manifestations of Universal values, except those that are inverted or severely misaligned, have the capacity for transmutation. It is assured that germinal and pure strain seeds can transmute, while hybrid or manipulated seeds may not. We also know that dualism will recede. At this time there is radical discontinuity between your inner essential and your outer material dimensions. Your development in one does not necessarily correspond with the other, leaving many among you material-rich and love-poor, or love-rich and material-poor. In your forthcoming expansion this integrity gap will close. Once this occurs, you will be able to work from the inside out or from the outside in, to produce growth throughout—replacing dualism with integralism. It is unlikely you will maintain a *priority* focus on the material level of your life. These are just a few of the probabilities for your future. Your planetary magnetism and frequency are changing even now. All organic forms are responding to the new field.

Earth is rapidly approaching the new millennium and the exploration of Universal integrity. This excites us and draws our focus toward physical reunion with you. We have already begun to reoccupy our black hole in your space/time, once again focusing our star for visibility in your heavens.

Do we who come from beyond
the Earth have superpowers like
Obewan Kenobe, Superman or Merlin?

*T*HERE ARE PEOPLE ON EARTH now who are capable of forms of self-expression that are extraordinary relative to the current state of Human development. Some of them are Cosmic Beings, living among you to inform you of Universality and to inform themselves of Humanity. Most of them are Human Beings who have reunified with their Soul and its resources. Their lives now demonstrate greater dimensions of what it means to be a person.

Your Soul is the manifestation of your frequency/value that is responsible for personalizations and the assumption of temporal forms. It interfaces and integrates the seminal state of your Being with the temporal individuated manifestations of your Being—of which you are one. Your Soul is the source from which your identity on Earth is generated. It expresses Universal nature and is possessed of Universal knowledge. All the wisdom your Soul contains is available to you when you align and merge with it. This reunion enables extraordinary capacities to integrate into your daily life on Earth.

Addressing just the physical level, I have seen Human Beings walk through walls, manifest foodstuffs, change shape, move great distances in an instant, appear in times past, and perform profound healings. There are also many people on Earth who are not fully aligned with their Soul, but who maintain an uncommon pathway of communication between particular dimensions of reality. This enables them to demonstrate psychic capacities.

It is important not to confuse the psychic who has an open pathway, with the Soul aligned Being who is an open pathway. The message of a medium is only as clear as the medium.

Transcendence of the practical and emotional realities of daily life on Earth is a shortcoming of most psychic counsel and interdimensional guidance. From my experience as a Being who enjoys life both on and off the Earth, I do not think it is possible to be nonlocal to Earth's reality system and understand the demands of its variability and its dualism. Living this lifetime on Earth I have a much greater appreciation for the Human challenge than I had when I was supporting you from the Cosmos.

Those of us who are facilitators of interdimensional communication demonstrate the extraordinary to varying degrees, depending upon our individual purposes and identities. I came to Earth to help build bridges of understanding between the multiple dimensions of self and Universe. I wanted to experience whether it is still possible to get here (Universal alignment) from there (Earth's current consciousness). So many people are seeking Universal love and knowledge and failing to find it, I wanted to understand why. For this reason I am using only the same capacities and skills that you embody. I have worked my way to Soul unification during this lifetime on Earth just as you would.

Because I am unified with my Soul resources I have what you might call "powers," but they are only an extension of resources you use every day. With my eyes I see exactly as you see, but I also see the heart of the matter. With my ears I hear just as you hear, but I also hear clearly that which is being left unsaid. With my body I experience myself and the world of forms, but I am also being constantly informed of the everchanging conditions of All That Is. I do have these powers, but they are simply the maturation of your known senses. They do not shelter me from the trials and conflicts of the daily world. Even without abracadabra, this fuller realization of Human senses is so empowering it can excite feelings of alchemy or power among those who experience it.

In the earlier years of this lifetime on Earth I was not using these natural powers because I did not know I had them—just as you may not know you have them. Most of you have yet to discover your multidimensional nature. You are working your way toward discernment of your inner voice and trust in your inner-direction. When you claim these connections, they will inspire courage of action. Then you will be able to experience and know your multi-dimensionality.

A key is self-love without judgement. Most people think they should be more than they are. Because they can imagine a *better* self, they implicitly believe they are a *lesser self*. If you could be the better self you imagine, you would be. Placing your value in a self you have yet to become devalues the self you already are. While today's self will not be sufficient for tomorrow, it is the best self you can be today and it is all the moment calls for. Seeing yourself as a mile from where you want to be may keep you from traveling the inch that is available to you at the moment.

There are no necessary exercises. There are no necessary techniques. There is nothing external you must do in order to grow into Soul alignment. While there is much you can learn from the discoveries and teachings of others, the nature of the Universe lives within you. By living fully the moment you are in, you will find yourself growing. You need only practice love, integrity, honesty and inner-directedness. If development of your higher potentials were dependent upon courses, programs or schools, this would be an elitist Universe. Only those with time, money and sophisticated intellectual skills could discover their potential. Consciousness does not work that way. Your life contains your teachings and your opportunities—if you trust it and live it fully.

If you believe others hold secrets that you do not, you will look there and find them there. When you come to a question that no one else can answer for you, you will have to transfer authority back to yourself and become your own resource. You are not likely to produce such a question until you are ready to trust yourself enough to surrender external authority. Your identity is never subjugated. Even when you use the paths of others, you have chosen them yourself. It is impossible to act without revealing your own nature.

Until you are liberated to trust your own inner-direction, your experience will be limited by your beliefs. Once you are liberated to follow your own inner-direction, your experience will shape your beliefs.

To discover and realize your powers and your nature as a Universal Being, meet the challenges of the moment honestly with choices that reflect the values and understanding you truly feel. By this action you will propel yourself toward enlightenment. It does not matter if what you felt to be your highest value turns out to be just another socially programmed idea or even a prideful, self-righteous notion. What matters is that you are willing to live it, to invest yourself in it, and to find out what it has to reveal to you about yourself and the nature of All That Is.

*How do things
come to be?*

*E*VERYTHING IN THE WORLD, and in the Universe, is made of the same basic stuff—*energy*. All energy is endowed with consciousness, but all energy does not demonstrate consciousness in the same way. Meanings and associations are demonstrations of Human consciousness. A rose also has consciousness. It interacts by receiving and broadcasting vibrational stimuli, just as people do, but it does not examine or make meaningful its process.

All energy is inherently capable of manifesting substantive forms— bodies, stars, ecosystems. All energy is also inherently capable of manifesting subtle forms—feelings, thoughts, planetary influences. Manifestation and reality are not dependent upon substantive form. They are dependent upon frequencies, values and consciousness.

Regardless of its state of Being, energy constellates in response to the stimuli of Universal values. These values—love, courage, compassion, trust and integralism, among them—underlie and transcend diversity. There is nothing more fundamental to being.

Each Universal frequency/value contains the whole and is contained within the whole, depending on your point of view within multidimensionality. As you read on, remember that *you* are a Universal frequency/value and the nature of these essential processes applies to you and your life experience.

All Universal values—embodied as you, me, trees, minerals, and all that comprises nature—are aspects of their Source that are manifest as autonomous identities. When a value is first expressed into creation as an individuated identity it demonstrates a frequency. The "birth" of a new frequency sends a stimulus into the Cosmos. All previously manifest frequencies resonate with this stimulus because the newborn frequency already lives within them, as undiscerned potential. Since each value is a reflection of its Creator in the moment of its creation, that which is not yet discerned within the Creator is not yet discerned within the creation. That which is undiscerned is present and essential to the whole, but it is indistinguishable, like a note in a symphonic movement. As a value becomes discerned and individuated within All That Is, it gains identification within all other manifest values. In this way a Universal value is inherently all-inclusive and self-expansive. It is energy in perpetual motion.

Each frequency/value is inherently magnetic, with an innate capacity for alignment with all other frequencies (Sympathetic Vibrational Magnetism). A frequency can attract energy to itself for alignment (stimulus, dynamicism) or be attracted by a stimulus sent out from another frequency (response, receptivity). Every time a frequency is born and sends out its stimulus, the magnetism of the Universe is activated. The Cosmos becomes awhirl with a dance of dynamicism and receptivity, as all that is manifest reorganizes and realigns to include the newborn value. Expressing an innate motivation for self-realization, each newborn value is attracted to its predecessors, circling and prodding them, seeking entry or union, intent upon awakening itself within them. Each predecessor, equally motivated toward realization, responds in turn to the stimulus of the new frequency, joining in the dance of circling and prodding. In its own pattern of orbit, each frequency traverses the orbits of the others—in the same way Earth, true to its own orbit, would come to traverse the orbit of the orbiting sun. So integral and equal is the nature of each value to the others that stimulus and response become indistinguishable in the mutuality of their desire to align themselves.

As a new frequency and its predecessors circle around one another, there is within each pairing a unique point where each is vibrationally sympathetic, or synchronous, with the other. Entry is possible at these points where each frequency is sympathetically aligned with its own value in the other. In the fulfillment of entry a merge occurs through which each value realizes itself in the other and ignites the other into greater self-realization. After merging, their orbits continue, each regaining its independence, profoundly informed by the other.

In this process of conjoining, each frequency gains attributes of manifestation as well as aspects of consciousness. By the time a frequency is aligned with all others, its manifestation can be expressed as energy, light, color, sound, movement, feeling or consciousness. In this way the Universe is ever-expanding, infinitely variable and continually integral.

Whether they are newborn or established, when values temporarily merge with one another, a fusion-like phenomena occurs, releasing free energy into the Cosmos. This produces a glorious flash of illumination, igniting each of the merging values into luminosity. The more a value merges with other aspects of its potential, the more luminous it becomes. This would be exquisite even if only one value were dancing its way through creation, but values are often born several in succession, in a stream, like streams of consciousness. When a stream of new frequencies comes into Being, the Cosmos resounds with the vibrational stimuli of its entry. It is a Universal OM. To this music all manifest values dance their dance of circling and prodding, bringing themselves to illumination in one another. The vibrations of their moving force resound in the revelation of harmonies. Trails of light draw pathways through the heavens as luminosities traverse the Cosmos to align and conjoin. Light dances and whirls through light in intricate patterns as shadings and shadows emerge from every nuance of movement. Everchanging vistas of design are shaped and disbanded as lumin-osities constellate in pursuit of alignment and bursts of resplendent energy announce their unions found. When each aspect of Creation has danced its dance and brought itself to light in all, a peaceful stillness permeates the Cosmos...until the Universe is stimulated into its next tarantella of integralism.

A dance of integralism happens within the Cosmos each time a value is discerned within All That Is and given expression in the Universe as an autonomous identity—a Being. It also happens within you, each time you discern a value within yourself and give it expression in the world. The dance of your personal integralism is not limited to the first time a value becomes self-evident. Each time you reconceive that value and expand your expression of it, a reconstellation of your energy is stimulated. Each reconstellation is an enlightenment and results in greater self-realization.

When you merge your awareness with your action and give expression to any value, you become magnetically charged with the frequency of that value. The union of your potential and your actuality releases a burst of luminosity that enhances the amplitude of your frequency and sends out a stimulus. The energy of the world and the Universe respond to the stimulus by delivering experiences that reflect, demonstrate and edify your self-realization. This is *Sympathetic Vibrational Magnetism* at work.

If you are disinclined to the technical do not be concerned. The ideas that follow will become clear to you in a forthcoming metaphor.

———————————————— ⌇⌇ ————————————————

All creations begin with a stimulus and proceed through processes of response, alignment and merging, before they become manifest. For you to create something, available energy must be magnetized by the stimuli broadcast from the frequencies and values inherent in your intention. Not all of the responding energy will align compatibly. Attempting to align, it will self-select in accordance with its ability to give expression to the discrete values within the gestalt that is your intention. The responding energy continues to self-select until the required mergings occur and a stable and self-perpetuating constellation of energy is achieved. As a result of your creative stimuli something has come to be.

The process of things coming to be may be more easily grasped in the metaphor of a choreographer who is creating a dance company for a theatrical production. There are thousands of trained dancers (*available energy*). To realize their potential they need to become part of a performance constellation (*a formulating creation*). The available dancers are waiting to hear of a production (*an organizing stimulus*) to try out for. Many of these dancers will find out about (*be magnetized to*) the choreographer's production. They will audition (*attempt to align themselves*) for the parts. Since in this case only jazz and acrobatic dancers (*discrete values*) are needed for the dance concept to be realized, most ballet dancers will not apply (*self-selection*).

Some ballet dancers with jazz experience may be among those to try out (*self-selection*). They will not necessarily be eliminated before auditions just because they are ballet dancers. One of them may bring just the right mix (*the right value and/or amplitude*) to give expression (*manifestation*) to a certain subtle quality within the choreographer's concept. Other dancers may find that they can qualify in jazz, but they do not want to dance it because they do not feel expressed (*properly aligned*) within it; they prefer ballet (*self-selection*).

The choreographer will hire (*constellate*) only those dancers who, in expressing their own capacities (*discrete values and amplitudes*), are successful in realizing his creative concept (*organizing stimulus*). He may continue to hire and fire dancers until the show opens, looking for the right combination of dancers to work well together as a unit (*a stable and self-perpetuating constellation of energy*). Once he has found a collective of talent that works together as a team (*discrete values successfully merged*), his production has found its life (*available energy formulates to manifest a reality*). A unique thing has come to be.

If the performers go beyond *alignment* and succeed in *merging* with one another in realization of their common intent, they will transcend their medium and stimulate themselves and their audience with the frequency of Creation itself. Such performances are recognized as transcendent and profound. They are directly healing to all who experience them.

The best dance company is one in which all dancers are fulfilling their individual values within the collective identity of the group. Any dancer who manipulates his or her value in order to fit into the group, will have difficulty with spontaneous adaptation when it is called for. Eventually that dancer will cease to conform and will catalyze change that may affect the stability of the group. It is not uncommon for a constellation of energy to include an unstable member in order to assure change or temporality of the constellation. This is highly advantageous to experimentation and self-realization, and often requisite to it. Constellations may also select unstable members as a reflection of misalignment in the creative concept, or the creator of the concept.

While your creation will express its own form, appearing within the world to be something other than you, actually it is more of you—in another state of being. Your creations formulate your identity into another expression of the Soul identity that formulated you (your Soul identity being another expression of the Source that formulated it). Your creation will embody and express your essential and measurable signature—your frequency/value, but it will broadcast your frequency/value into the world through the attributes of its own manifest state, rather than yours.

As expressions of your frequency and value, your creations will vary only in their amplitude, reflecting your immediate state of being at the time of their creation. Whether you create a bridge, an opera or a flower, each will manifest its own constant energy pattern— its own form—embodying your frequency/value. Each will also manifest its own variability of amplitude. The frequency amplitude of the bridge will change under different conditions of stress and maintenance. The frequency amplitude of the opera will change with each company that performs it and with each performance by that company. The frequency amplitude of the flower will change relative to its environmental conditions and its stage of life. So long as your creations maintain integrity with All That Is and with the amplitude levels appropriate to their reality system, your frequency/value continues to broadcast from them.

No one can know the full range of manifestations that will result from their creative stimuli. No one knew what a tulip, rose, acorn, elm tree or walrus would look like until its axial value stimulated all other values into a collective pattern that stabilized, revealing its form relative to the Earth. No Being knew what a Human Being would look like until the organization of values comprising a Human Being formulated to produce one. In another context of reality, a Human Being could configure as a spiral light body with omnidirectional eyes or as a comet-like luminosity.

The value that you embody and express is not the only expression of you in the world or the Universe. There are numerous manifestations of you. Your value may also be expressed as a mineral, an element, an organic process, an aroma, a seaweed, a psychological capacity, a layer of facia, a geological pattern, a cultural attribute or a fish. The African Violet you so love, and your dear friend from childhood, may be two manifestations of the same Being. Even if they are worlds apart, each manifestation of a value can stimulate self-realization within the others.

Your scientists and metaphysicians may appreciate the implications of this in relation to morphic fields and morphic resonance: the passing of formative casual influences across space and time.

Each constellation of energy—a tree, a rock, an idea or even a dream—is the manifestation of a value or a unique combination of values. Most people are not yet sufficiently attuned to actually see the light and color, hear the sound waves or recognize the discrete values that compose the people, things and feelings around them. As Humanity comes to be so tuned in the years ahead, all things will participate in your dialogue with the Universe. Not only will the most mundane things around you reveal themselves to be responsive and multidimensional, but every Being you meet —Human or otherwise—will be revealed as a profound creator of reality.

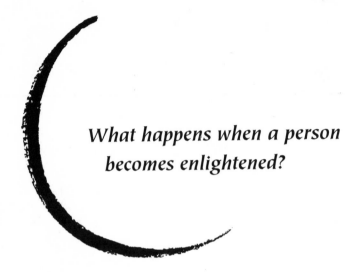

*What happens when a person
becomes enlightened?*

*I*T IS NOT EASY TO BE A SEEKER, but neither is it easy to be a finder. Because of Humanity's confusion and misalignment of values, the world is a hard place to live for any loving and sensitive Being—seeker or finder.

Once you are a finder, all becomes knowable and seeking becomes meaningless. In surrendering the tenacious drive to seek, you are freed to experience the graces of enlightenment that live in the moment. Knowing what to look for and how to see, the material world no longer obscures essential reality. Whatever is relevant, regardless of its placement in the multidimensionality of space, time and being, is clearly revealed to you.

Enlightenment calls you to accustom yourself to the internal quietude of knowing rather than the clamoring tension of questioning. This transition changes your rhythms of being. In the new rhythms of enlightenment, all the Universe flows through you and you are effortlessly informed of the potential of each moment. So informed, you are empowered to facilitate the realization of this potential in ways the moment itself reveals to you.

An individual who develops to self-realization, or enlightenment, does not become purposeless or transcendent of personal passions. Individual identity continues to self-express, realizing potentials born from other dimensions of its Being—dimensions beyond those currently characteristic of Humanity.

Enlightenment is the realization of a Human Being's capacity for physical, emotional, psychological, intellectual, transpersonal and spiritual integrity, both individually and in synchronistic cooperation with the capacity of all other Human Beings to so express. Enlightenment does not mean that all things ever to be known and felt are already known and felt. Rather, it means that you have merged with the Universal nature and resources of your Soul, and that you are fully available to the potential aspiring to realization in any given moment.

With enlightenment life is enriched and the problems of each level are availed of the resolving wisdom of the next. You are liberated to enjoy multidimensionality within the repetitive maintenance of the mundane: chopping wood and carrying water. There is no resistance, no manipulation, no need for control, nothing to block you from being constantly informed of the everchanging nature of All That Is. You have mastered the capacity to understand yourself and live in the moment, unencumbered by past attachments or future projections. This is often misinterpreted as living free of the material world and its responsibilities. In fact, it is the ability to live free *within* the material world and its responsibilities. Just as contrived materialism can consume the spirit, contrived spirituality can consume the fullness of material experience.

One who is preoccupied with yesterday's experience is not available to be informed by today's Universe. Being current with yourself is the posture of enlightenment. This is the alchemy of yoga. Enlightenment is a timeless transmission from one's Soul, a gift from one's Source, and an ongoing process of attuning consciousness. If you are current with yourself, your body and your body of thought are available to be informed of the evolving and changing nature of the world and the Universe. When your spectrum of response ability is as broad as your multidimensional nature, without effort you find yourself knowing the state of being of anything you focus upon. This knowing comes through your own life form, through your body, its senses, your daily experience and your multidimensional inner resources. When you inhabit your form in this way your consciousness is constantly receiving the latest news and ideas. While journals or papers may be of interest to you there is no need to read them, except to see how other people are interpreting what is changing in your collective reality. As an enlightened Being you are continually updated on the state of the union. You know directly what is changing because it is changing *you*.

If you are enlightened in relation to the world, your horizons expand to include other dimensions of Universal reality. When these are realized and integrated, more dimensions reveal themselves. Realization is the making real of that which is potential —and potential is endless.

Because of their capacity to manifest potential, those who are enlightened are often experienced as powerful—and indeed they are. True power results from the alignment of Human will with Universal nature. In this state your power demonstrates effortlessly.

It is the nature of energy to be responsive. Energy does not discriminate with regard to content. Any time you focus and direct energy toward a creative end, you are aligning your Human will with the energy of Creation and you will experience some measure of empowerment. You may feel and express this empowerment as strength, direction or validation; or you may feel and express it as control, powerfulness or superiority. Whether your will focuses and directs creatively toward something born from all-serving inspiration or something born from self-serving manipulation, the superficial experience is the same: empowerment. Regardless of the content or morality of your action, the creative application of will gives you a feeling of personal power.

Whether you are ruled by your ego or served by your ego is your choice. Values and integrity are for the individual to discern. Therein lies enlightenment—the only true and lasting power. Aspiring to control rather than to Universal alignment, or to personal gain rather than to collective integrity, are parts of the same process at different amplitude levels of consciousness and love. Eventually the self-serving self uses up the satisfactions of power and feels the desire for love. When this happens, power redefines to the Universal level and a life that was trapped in circles of power is liberated into spirals of empowerment.

Nature, being discerning but not discriminating, does not hold a Universal self or a Soul in greater esteem than a personal self. That is why creativity generated from either level is empowering. Each dimension of self has the capacity to inform the others. Ultimately, it is the full realization of the relationship between personal self and Universal self that produces ego liberation and enlightenment.

In esoteric teachings you may experience or learn of enlightened Masters who have the capacity to manifest themselves in more than one place at one time. The material body participates in one place, while the energy/light body participates in another. Bi-location is not a metaphor. It is a real occurrence. This ability results naturally from full realization of an *equal* relationship between the personal self and the Soul. When this equality exists, each aspect brings its own nature into the form of the other. When each aspect of self has, through time and experience, successfully informed the other of its nature, each fully includes the capacities of the other. This empowers each to participate in the domain of the other. Your Earthly self can transcend its form and participate in the realm of your Soul, and your Soul's energy/light body can assume your worldly form and participate in the earthly domain. It is also possible for both aspects of a Being to appear simultaneously in the same domain. These are all demonstrations of alchemical syntropic power. While conscious bi-location is currently an extraordinary capacity for most Human Beings, it is a natural result of the unification of personal self and Universal Soul. While it cannot be taught or learned, it can be practiced and refined once it emerges naturally. Not to be confused with this phenomena of bi-location, there are processes such as *remote viewing* that can be learned and are not dependent upon integrity or enlightenment.

You may think that self-mastery and enlightenment result from superior capacities that set the Masters apart from you. This is not so. They have successfully met no greater challenges than you meet daily. A Master, or an enlightened Being, is one who fully knows his or her self. Since each of us contains All That Is, there is nothing beyond or outside of the self to master.

In the state of enlightenment, or self-mastery, you are an alchemist. Transformations result within or without the confines of space and time, from your ability to transmute and facilitate energy. Because you are able to see what is possible in each moment, you can consciously facilitate possibility into actuality. You can do all of this in relation to the world because you can do all of this within yourself.

Since creativity and power are both available regardless of morality, how do your acts of will and power on Earth affect the rest of the Universe? In every way and in some ways not at all. All the Universe is cooperative in one circulatory system of being. Every moment that expresses full potential anywhere in the Universe is experienced everywhere in the Universe as a fulfillment and a vitalization. Your embrace of life, your expression of love and your aspiration to self-realization are essential to the circulatory system of All That Is. This is life feeding itself.

Any moment in which you express less than your potential is not nourishing to the Greater Universe, but neither is it damaging. Finding no alignment with Universal integrity, these expressions lose coherence in the Universal system. While such expressions rarely impact the Universal system, they can impact an individual's personal and collective reality.

Everyone needs the personal freedom to create their own reality and means of learning, even when the impact of their power appears self-serving. We who currently enjoy more enlightened systems than yours have had this privilege. All of us have learned by doing. All of us have indulged ourselves in order to learn. So long as you do not violate another's freedoms, no one has the right to judge your personal and collective processes of exploration and development. Rest assured that the enlightenment of one Human Being illuminates far more than the confusion of many can obscure.

Universal enlightenment is an experience that transcends anything imaginable. It engages you in direct experience of *yourself as the Universe.* Miraculously, the creation of the Universe recapitulates in you, informing you of All That Is and how it has come to be. Enlightenment is not an end. It is a gift, a grace born of self-realization…a moment of transformation between formations.

*Is it possible to transcend subjectivity
and see things as they really are?*

WHILE SUBJECTIVITY can be limiting, it is not something that need be remedied. Subjectivity enables you to make use of a lifetime as a medium for self-expression, rather than as a vehicle for matriculating through the accumulated constructions of others.

———————— ⌒⌒ ————————

Subjectivity is an endowment of All That Is. It enables you to be the creator of your own life experience by allowing you to empower objects and situations with infinite variability and meanings. It facilitates creativity and supports individuality. While your subjectivity is unique to you, subjectivity is within the potential to all Beings. It is a Universal value.

———————— ⌒⌒ ————————

The capacity to empower objects and situations with subjective meanings is an inherent mechanism for self-healing. It enables you to spontaneously heal something that may have happened many years ago. Picture yourself walking through the woods. The sun is playing checkers with the treetops and a soft wind brings you a waft of wild sage. At the moment you become aware of the sage, you are looking down at your red sneakers. Without being conscious of it, you are reproducing the combination of elements surrounding a situation that impacted you when you were a child in your grandmother's kitchen. Your grandma, in a red apron, was cooking a sage turkey dressing. A breeze from the open kitchen window sent the aromas wafting through the house as the sun was making patches on the kitchen floor—and at just that moment, something painful happened to you.

Sympathetic Vibrational Magnetism gives you the capacity to effortlessly reconfigure the variables of a past moment and align them with subjective meaning. A conscious or subconscious need to heal the incident in grandma's kitchen led you to reconstruct the sensory variables of the incident. But did wearing red sneakers on the walk through a breezy sage-filled woods stimulate the healing opportunity, or did the need for healing stimulate you to plan the walk through a breezy sage-filled wood and choose your red sneakers? In multidimensional events, Universal simultaneity often overrides local time or practical sequence. It is nearly impossible to know which factor is the stimulus and which is the response.

When you recreate the variables of a past moment of experience your current subjectivity costumes them in such a way that the historic incident need not be apparent. The synthesis of frequencies from the historic moment realigns you with the energy of that moment, providing an opportunity for healing and regeneration of the values that were originally impacted.

Is it possible to transcend subjectivity and see things as they really are?

The process is entirely subjective. Whether you are conscious or unconscious of having invoked the old, you are enabled by subjectivity to imbue its variables with new meanings. The way you internalize the stimuli of the new moment can transform the pain and significance of the old, creating a moment of spontaneous healing. This is the alchemy of spontaneous self-healing. It happens frequently throughout your life, although usually without your awareness.

~~~

If you entertain this idea in the multidimensional context of Soul memory, the deepest referent for the red shoes may be an experience within your Soul of a more primitive culture, where a red string on the ankle marked you for death. While your conscious mind might locate the painful memory in your grandma's kitchen, what caused the event in your grandma's kitchen to be so painful may have been your Soul memory of the red string.

Every perspective is a lens for viewing that automatically limits your perception to its particular power of magnitude. Every complex system of energy is made up of smaller subsystems, each possessing its own stimuli, magnetism and organization of values. On Earth, people usually experience only the gestalt of these subsystems. When you greet someone you get an overall feeling. You do not feel the vibration of what was eaten for breakfast, distinct from the vibration of an angelic night's sleep, or from the vibration of kidney function. These discrete vibrations communicate themselves just as clearly as the gestalt vibration—if you have the presence of perception. You can perceive any moment of experience with a microscope, a magnifying glass, a zoom lens or a telescope.

No matter what you perceive to be the larger system, there is always one larger, always one smaller. You think the cell lives in the kidney and the kidney lives in the body. This is true. Within what, then, does the body live?

All that lives within any perspective you believe to be subjective is actually measurable and has objective values at its root. Energy, frequency, vibration, magnetism and consciousness are all objective realities. They are not inherently subjective. What leads you to believe they are subjective is that their objective nature can be perceived only when it is *sympathetic* with the observer. Only if you know your own mind is it possible to perceive the essential nature of what is before you. To the extent that you do not know the content and the impact of your own mind, there is room for projection and distortion. Once you are able to measure the objective reality of what is now seemingly subjective, the distortions of your own mind will no longer be invisible to you. They, too, will become measurable.

While the idea of measuring the invisible may seem futuristic, there are numerous examples in the everyday world of tools that do just that. Your home satellite dish captures invisible signals from the air and converts them to the sound and the images on your television. The invisible humidity in the air is measured with a psychrometer and reported by your weatherman. Musical instruments such as a guitar, horn or Scottish bagpipe, are tuned to a meter which reads their invisible sound frequencies.

In addition, there are many examples of complex medical technologies that measure invisible physiological signals and create images of the inner workings of the body. Among these are the electroencephalogram (EEG), magnetic resonance imaging (MRI), and computerized axial tomography (CAT Scan). You also have numerous less technical means for measuring the objective nature of vibrations. While these means could dramatically improve your resources for health and healing, they are being met with scientific resistance that inhibits the research and development necessary to validate them in your context. Crystals, pendulums, auric photography and biofield spectrum analyzers are all being used to read vibrations with varying levels of accuracy. Although some of these tools are older than science, they are currently considered too subjective to be respected as scientifically reliable.

Despite the popular debate concerning the intrinsic nature of subjectivity and the existence of objective reality, the Cosmic view affirms both subjective and objective reality. Their relationship becomes self-evident when multidimensionality is embraced.

Technologies for the unification of subjective and objective reality are currently being pioneered within your existing scientific model. They will serve the rebirthing of science that awaits you just across the threshold of the new millennium. One of the more innovative of these emerging technologies is a bioenergetic measurement tool recently developed by a master kinesiologist from the University of California. Her tool makes it possible for bodily vibrations to be measured as substantive reality. Its underlying concepts could change the face of diagnosis and healing in Western civilization. The model this tool provides for practical application of multidimensional information exemplifies the efforts of a wave of scientists who are already working in an integral, multidimensional and energy-based paradigm to launch your future science.

As a facilitator of interdimensional communication, I am not inhibited by the confines of your local science. The language within which your scientists must currently document their work is not big enough for their discoveries or for the Universal realities those discoveries are approaching. Physicists are bound to reconcile their views of the Universe with physical reality. To cross that boundary would put them in the domain of theological faith, which has no greater capacity than science to discern objective reality. Each of these realities—the physical and the theological—is incomplete and encompassed in a larger one. When I discuss Universal values and their essential objectivity, I am referring to this larger reality.

Everything in the Universe is based on essential building blocks: frequencies, values, magnetism. Regardless of where we are in the Greater Universe, we all work with the same frequencies and values. This is what enables interdimensional and interspecies communication. Only the prioritization of these frequencies and values differs, relative to the nature of each reality system. Illusion, confusion and misconception occur when these building blocks get inverted or misaligned in the course of reality construction—and no one corrects it.

As you consider what follows, be careful not to limit yourself to the popular view of values as having ethical or moral implications. I am discussing Universal values as essential and objective states more fundamental than your popular conception of values.

───────────────◦◦◦───────────────

Every thing, feeling, thought, idea, Being or condition that has ever been or will ever be, has an essential frequency as its organizing principle. Each frequency has its own unique

Is it possible to transcend subjectivity and see things as they really are?

value. Like a signature, the frequency pattern of a value always looks the same, every time it appears, everywhere in the Universe. The value of a frequency is both conceptual and quantifiable. Since the quantifiable nature of any value is constant and measurable, it can be represented mathematically. The conceptual nature of any value is also constant, but subjectivity can interfere with its recognition. The variability in any frequency or value will exhibit in its measurable amplitude, reflecting how fully it is manifest in any instance, relative to its potential.

A frequency is a fundamental Universal stimulus, a seminal life force. The vibrations of a frequency are its local broadcast signal. Consciousness is their medium.

Courage is a vibrational frequency which demonstrates its value both conceptually and measurably. If you took a picture of the energy field when courage is being embodied or outwardly expressed by anyone, anywhere in the Universe, the same frequency pattern would always appear in the field. There is no ambiguity. Courage is measurable. The frequency pattern of courage is an objective reality. The variabilities of courage will be reflected in the vibrational *amplitude* of the frequency each time it is expressed, not in its signature pattern. Its amplitude will vary according to how fully courage is manifest in any instance, relative to the potential of that moment. While ambivalence or reticence will cause courage to demonstrate a low amplitude, fully expressed courage will demonstrate such a high amplitude that all would recognize it and commonly name it.

In an ideal configuration of variables, courage would manifest the full amplitude of its nature—its absolute, or objective, state. When philosophers debate whether everything is relative (a current popular view), or whether there are absolutes (a historic popular view), they are grappling with the multidimensional nature of frequencies and values. Frequencies are absolute, but within unenlightened subjective contexts the variables rarely configure to reveal them as such. Those who have cultivated rich internal experience, through meditation or other mediums of expanded response ability, are likely to have met absolute values as states of being.

Human Beings do not yet comprehend values as measurable. Frequencies are understood to be measurable, but it has not yet become clear to you that values are frequencies, and that frequencies are conceptual as well as quantifiable values. You currently understand values as conceptual. The conceptual thought form at the root of a value is as objective a reality as its measurable frequency, but because it is currently perceived through meaning rather than measure, it is subject to interpretation. It is in your subjective interpretation that values become saddled with morality and judgement.

Courage has been used as an example. Patience, perseverance, conformity, individuality, discernment, empathy, order, confluence, clarity, alignment, subjectivity, receptivity, dynamicism, unification, transformation and whimsy, are other examples of values that express their own unique and constant frequency patterns. There is no end to the list. If you can think of it, it is a value, a combinant value, an inverted value or a misaligned value. When Humanity opens the discussion of values and frees them from the assignment of morality or judgement, you will have collectively embarked upon a path to peace, unity and Universal knowledge.

Universal frequencies are seminal forces. They are like Earth's germinal strains from which an unlimited number of combinations can be derived. A seminal frequency demonstrates a single value. A combination of seminal frequencies results in a formula of values, much like a recipe. Spirituality is a seminal frequency. Organization is another. Their combination can manifest as religion. The frequency patterns of spirituality and organization will both be evident in the frequency pattern of religion. Anything that exists can be traced to its seminal frequencies.

There was a time when it was inconceivable that one might measure what now comprises the Periodic Table of Elements. The fundamental elements of reality that you now interpret and believe to be subjective—courage, health, devotion, empathy—are actually as measurable as copper, uranium and hydrogen. The Universal values that are currently invisible to you are no different. They too will eventually become measurable.

Imagine how life would be if you could measure values physically and experience them empirically through higher development of your senses. You would know the extent to which a person with whom you are interacting has developed their integrity, generosity, empathy, physical health or emotional stability. You would know if you are being appreciated, manipulated, ignored or understood.

When a person's behavior does not match vibrational reality, you would have the perception to recognize the disparity, appreciate the intentions and identify the real conditions at play.

You will not lose your subjectivity and enter an objective world when you learn to identify values and measure the invisible. What will change is that people will no longer be ignorant of their projections upon other people and situations. The intentions of others will be evident in the values and frequency amplitudes they are demonstrating. There will be no place for manipulation and illusion. Intention will become transparent. With this recognition of values you can free yourself from unreasonable expectation. Your energy can be focused on creating yourself, your planetary community and more satisfying relationships—on Earth and beyond.

When it becomes readily apparent that even the most highly developed or admired people are works-in-progress, any notion of superiority and inferiority will dissolve. When both the greatness and the smallness in each person is readily recognizable, an equalizing will occur that will refound your humanity. Judgments will be more easily replaced with compassion and support. Your understanding of reality will change as a result of this embrace. You will recognize that you are all working on the same challenge in different ways and that no one is working against it. You will be able to see the opportunity provided by almost any situation, instead of perceiving it as random occurrence, bad luck, good fortune or the inheritance of others' mistakes.

Is it possible to transcend subjectivity and see things as they really are?

Some of you will awaken today and some tomorrow. An Age of Inspired Realism is already unleashed. It will be present for you when you are present for it. Knowingly or unknowingly, your society is already collectively engaged in the transmutation of its subjectivity.

Why do people get sick,
   have diseases, and experience pain?

*T*HE PEOPLE OF EARTH have come to a unique juncture in their planetary history. Already launched into a new paradigm and poised on the cusp of planetary *transmutation*, many people are experiencing manifestations of disease that would not otherwise be prevalent. The conditions that enable your eventual transmutation into a more expansive state of being also enable a unique spectrum of disintegrations, including auto-immune system dysfunctions.

There are two profound changes in progress in the nature of your planet that temporarily heighten your physical vulnerability, while producing the alchemical conditions for planetary transmutation into a more enlightened state of being: A change in Earth's frequency amplitudes and a change in Earth's magnetism. Both are well underway.

The increasing amplitude of Earth's frequencies moves everything, including you, just a hair more quickly...and then another hair more quickly...and another. Your cells and your consciousness are entrained by this planetary phenomenon. The entrainment is integrous. Its medium is *Sympathetic Vibrational Magnetism*. Because of this planetary increase in vibrational amplitude, you are likely to feel that there is not enough time to maintain the reality you constructed at a lesser amplitude, perhaps just a year ago. When your frequency raises to a higher vibrational amplitude, it puts you into resonance with aspects of both local and Universal reality that were previously unrecognized by you. This adds new dimensions, dynamics and relationships to your existing awareness—without increasing your time for integrating or exploring them. At the most mundane level this means that in every ten minutes spent washing your hair, what you are thinking about and processing within your energy field has increased in quantity, dimensionality and integralism, causing you to feel a relative lessening of time.

There are many factors contributing to the destabilization of time. Computer technology and other electronic media are stimulating alterations in the rhythms of Human synapses, expectations and interactions. The rhythms of your active day and resting night are not aligned with the clock, nor are they aligned with your planetary nature. And, the rotation of the Earth is slowing down.

With time destabilizing and consciousness expanding, it is no wonder so many people feel overwhelmed, rushed, and increasingly aware that their current way of life is unnatural. These intensifications are transitional impacts of the increasing vibrational amplitude of Earth's frequencies. There will be a point where this complexity transforms into profound

Why do people get sick, have diseases and experience pain?

simplicity and a new rhythm of being. Depending upon how global the scope of this syntropy is, this point of simplicity can be a personal or collective enlightenment, a transformation or a transmutation of consciousness.

———— ～～ ————

Those who are intimate with the rhythms of harmony, gracefulness and beauty will be among the first to recognize this change in frequency amplitudes and to align with it. Simplicity is key to this adjustment. Those who are being rewarded for their ability to maintain performance amidst the escalating demands of increasing complexity, will be slower to align with the change that is underway.

Concurrent with this change of frequency amplitude, Earth is progressing in a change of *magnetism*. It is Earth's magnetism that holds your ideas and perception tightly together as a relatively impermeable reality system. Without collective magnetism there would be no momentum behind ideas and concepts that experience demonstrates to be faulty. Without constancy of planetary magnetism you would regularly experience bleedthroughs to other reality systems and other dimensions of your own reality. Also, without a constancy of magnetism you would not be able to attract the energy needed to convert an idea or intention into a manifest reality.

———— ～～ ————

In the current transitional phase of your transmutational process, Earth's magnetism is breaking down. It is becoming more penetrable in order to enable new coordinates of magnetism and new amplitudes of frequency to instate. This means that when you broadcast a stimulus that is endemic to the dissolving paradigm, the receiving context itself—the world—is less coherent. Because there is less coherence there is increased opportunity for interference between stimulus and response.

Since it is the nature of a transmutational process to draw energy from the dissolving system into resonance with the forming system, not only will creating anything consistent with the old system become harder and harder, but there will be less and less energy available to it. At the same time, creating anything that is resonant with the emerging reality system will become easier and easier as more planetary energy is transmuted and becomes available to respond at the new level. Simply put, it will get harder to successfully consume hope and other natural resources or to express greed, competition, control and separatism.

As individuals integrate the increasing amplitude of their axial frequencies, and of all frequencies that constitute their reality, their insight and behavior will further align with Universal values. Such a population will change the social environment and, eventually, what is called "reality."

———————— ∽∾ ————————

This has been happening for more than half a century and it will progress over the coming years at an accelerated rate, until critical mass if realized. The phenomena of amplitude increase and magnetic decrease have not gone unobserved by those who measure frequency and magnetism, but there has been no conceptual context in which to make these observations meaningful.

Transformation is the capacity of an integral system to change structure and behavior without changing its nature.

Transmutation is the capacity of an integral system to change structure and behavior so fundamentally that it reveals different aspects of nature. This can include transfiguration, as well as the manifestation of new forms. Transmutation is a reorganization of values that redirects the energy of an entire reality system. The system and all of its potentials propel into a new state of integrity, through means that transcend both the surrendered and the newly embodied state.

The phenomenon of transmutation is already displayed within the nature of the Earth, in the proliferation of imaginal cells that finally take over and transmute caterpillar to butterfly. Those of you who embody the axial values or increased frequency amplitudes critical to each process of Human transformation, are Humanity's imaginal cells. Individually you may be resisted by the caterpillar as foreign invaders, but together you are its transmutational force and its survival.

When you who embody and express the values of the future come together to effect a common purpose, you will be irresistible. The caterpillar will surrender to transformation. Humanity and its reality will change form without dying. Until your consciousness is collectively coherent, however, the caterpillar will continue to try to fight you off, defending its survival as if you were a cancer.

In contemplating the idea of transmutation, consider the example of the red-spotted newt. Born in the water, equipped for water life, it later grows to develop a entire system of physical resources and functions that enable it to live on the land. These resources were not apparent in the waterborne newt and, interestingly, they do not replace the systems necessary for function as water life. The two systems maintain simultaneous integrity.

Transmutation is an alchemical phenomenon—a Universal grace. It has two prerequisite phases: transition and trans-formation. The transitional phase is a period of subtle conceptual and energetic change, during which awareness expands, values reorganize and consciousness elevates. The transitional phase gives birth to the transformational phase. In the transformational phase, these subtle changes become manifest. Purposeful action is taken to form and apply alli-ances and models that demonstrate elevated amplitudes of consciousness and a new organization of values. Humanity is currently moving into the transformational phase.

As the process progresses, fewer people will hold as *reality* the ideas and beliefs that currently govern your civilization. When new models for security emerge, people will feel safe acknowledging that what they have always called "reality" is just one set of choices from the menu of possibilities. With this acknowledgment, the externalization of values and the externalization of authority will diminish. Inner-direction and inner-authority will gain governance over individual and social reality. The reclaiming of authority from dysfunctional systems will enable new societal systems to emerge, consistent with Universal values and facilitated by those who embody those values with integrity.

Those of you who have spent the better part of your life working toward the transformation ahead, take solace—the window is opening. There is no need to push it. The resistance of old and unenlightened ways is not an obstacle; it provides critical controls to the rhythms of transformation. Humanity must be able to survive this process without the breakdown of all physical bodies, and without dissolution into personal and social chaos. Those who overpower or devalue your efforts, or who write you off as "power- less," "immature," or "idealistic," are not your adversaries. They are your collective immune system—empowered by the same values that empower your individual immune systems. Like *the hair of the dog that bit you,* their entrenchment in resistance, dualism and control serves you at this juncture. You cannot afford to have the new invading culture—no matter how elevated or Universal— consume your old body politic, your old body of thought, or your old three-dimensional bodies...not quite yet. You are not yet pre- pared to replace them. The consciousness of the future is already functioning among you, but it has not yet been successfully form- ulated for societal embodiment. The future is still developing, using the resources of the current, unenlightened collective body.

While you do not yet have new models and collectives in place to sustain the life and creative function of a Universally aligned, integral society, *you are not far from it.* Recognizing the need for transformation and sensing that the process is being supported by Universal forces, many of you have steadily progressed in identify- ing the conceptual framework and defining the values of an integral

Human society that honors the spiritual equality of all life. You are steadily gaining numbers, methods, alliances, recognition of your visionary thinkers and readiness for practical applications. Your ability to found a new world springs from your own internal transformations of consciousness and your own struggles to fully manifest this consciousness in the world.

All of this transformational work is critical to transmutation—the quantum fruition of this movement. But your momentum is not yet engaged. You have not yet identified yourselves as the massive collective you are—the emerging transformational culture. You have not yet recognized the vastness of your number and collectivized to satisfy your basic needs. When you identify your resources and address yourselves to integral systems for accommodating your fundamental needs, you will stimulate the individual trust necessary to bond you as a collective. This will expedite transformative action and unleash Universal momentum.

You need working transformative models. Get practical. Provide enlightened options for satisfying primary needs. Transcending your current economic model, establish systems for providing yourselves with bio-dynamic or organically produced food; simplified, aesthetic and environmentally compatible individual and collective housing; all-inclusive, integral healthcare; and live forums for the transformative dialogue. This will create positive public awareness and a popular desire to change the existing system, bit by bit. Divert the potential for social chaos by enlisting conscious public commitment to a cycle of social transformation. People will rise to transformational action once effective noncompetitive models for the maintenance of survival are available.

When the coherence of magnetism breaks down and the opportunity for interference increases, not only does business-as-usual get increasingly difficult and the body politic become transparent, but the physical body itself becomes more vulnerable to interference. The immune system is less able to defend itself within a context that is becoming increasing permeable because of the diminishing coherence of magnetism. The weakening boundaries of your reality system support permeation of some cellular boundaries and weaken certain individual immune systems. Since you are transitional and still dualistic in your nature, transmutational energy manifests in your system as both a strength and a weakness. Those who are giving their lives to this process through cancer, AIDS and numerous other diseases, are surrendering to temporal personal loss in order to realize collective Human gain.

The dysfunctions of life as you currently know it are being consumed by an emerging culture with emerging integrity. Naturally the system will fight against its demise; it is a dualistic system. An immune system functions on the premise that all is not one, that forces of change are invaders rather than transformers of life, and that the reigning system is superior to any other.

Healers and their healing arts are currently extending the coherent consciousness of many people who are dying, availing them of enlivened rather than drugged states in which to do the work of completing a life cycle and embracing transmutation. This healing work honors unseen dimensions of the dying person, often aligning the person with experience of these dimensions while she or he is still alive. You have created the hospice to support conscious dying, and a resurgence of midwifery to support conscious birthing. Both hospicing and midwifery focus the energy of transition on personal growth, Universal alignment and the integrity of natural process. What is needed next is a framework, supported by healers and facilitators, that provides your civilization with an opportunity to focus its collective transition process toward these same ends— personal and collective growth, Universal alignment, and the integrity of natural process. Call in the midwives. What is before you is a natural birth crisis. It *will* be a labor. It *can* be a labor of love.

While phenomenal planetary and Universal influences are unfolding, you still have immediate and established personal concerns in regard to sickness, disease and pain. Because many of these concerns will not dissolve until the paradigm that supports them dissolves, information that has more immediate and practical application may be useful to you.

In the process of embracing responsibility for creating your own reality, a misconception has been perpetuated among you. People are interpreting their power as creators to include responsibility for illnesses that have been genetically programmed through previous generations. Fueled by the human inclination toward guilt, this misconception is difficult to unravel. As individuals you are no more responsible for such illnesses than you are for the fact that you eat candy and get cavities and someone else eats candy and does not. Your responsibility begins when it becomes clear that you are cavity prone. Then do you stop eating candy?

Factors of genetic inheritance and environmental provocation are beyond your singular responsibility. What is within your responsibility is sickness or *dis-ease* that results from separations you create or allow to remain within yourself. You can separate from yourself physically, emotionally, psychologically, intellectually, transpersonally or spiritually. These are the aspects that comprise your Human identity. Any separation puts you in an adversarial relationship with yourself. In an adversarial relationship someone always gets hurt; someone always suffers. If you are fighting against yourself, who is going to lose?

Separating or excluding any aspect of your identity from the rest of yourself is a rejection of your nature that creates a break in your life flow. As long as your overall identity can compensate for the break you will not manifest noticeable signs of illness or disease. Your body has sufficient tolerances to temporarily sustain stress from experimentation that fosters your maturity and self-realization. If you no longer have the resources to sustain the stress of separation, the discontinuity of energy flow will result in breakdown: illness or disease.

While you may suffer until you recreate integrity among the many aspects of your identity, your body will cooperate in the regeneration of your nature. Even when that cooperation is expressed as death, it is part of a larger regenerative process. If a person's frequency/value cannot be expressed without a greater resource of health, the body cooperates by completing its cycle to enable the Being to reorganize and regenerate. As your capacities for transmutation become vitalized, you will eliminate this cause of death. Allowing for death and regeneration as healing mediums, the resources for healing any dysfunctional manifestation exist within the multidimensional framework of your own identity.

The ancient Chinese art of acupuncture provides a model for under-standing the multidimensional relationships of well-being and dis-ease. In acupuncture, each aspect of your well-being has its own energy pathway called a *meridian*. When a meridian cannot regu-late its flow properly, it either shuts down or borrows energy from another meridian. Unless the balance rights itself as a result of this borrowing, the lender will become a borrower—and on and on until the entire system is in arrears. Acupuncture identifies the energy imbalance and facilitates the pathways so the energy can reinstate, or equalize, itself. It relies entirely upon the inherent multidimen-sional resources and integrity of body consciousness. When the initial cause of the borrowing has stopped withdrawing from the collective bank account there is self-correction.

In the perspective of acupuncture, each case of arthritis, asthma, allergy or other specific illness, is recognized as being the effect of a unique pattern of cause. Numerous different pathologies of borrowing and lending could be identified as the same illness. Acupuncture focuses on reinstating energy balance rather than on the condition an imbalance produces. Like a question conceived in confusion that dissolves without being answered once the con-fusion has passed, the illnesses and conditions resulting from energy imbalance dissolve when energy becomes aligned. This alchemy is not exclusive to the practice of acupuncture. Homeo-pathy and numerous other healing arts are founded on such multidimensional understanding.

Cause and effect relationships of illness or disease are most visible when they occur within the same aspect of your identity. When a dirty object punctures your skin and pollutes your tissue or blood-stream, an infection occurs. When you fall skiing, your leg breaks if your body cannot compensate for the stresses incurred. These are examples of physical effects of *physical* causes.

It is more difficult to recognize and provide health care for the *emotional* and *psychological* separations within your nature that result in physical manifestations. Breaking a leg in a skiing fall has a more obvious connection than breaking a leg in a skiing fall because of a broken heart. If your commitments require your full attention when you are longing to retreat, grieve and renew a broken heart, your separation from your psychological and emotional integrity may break your physical leg. When you are in respectful possession of your emotional and psychological needs there is no need for the device of displacement. You can choose to stop the unnatural life pace of your world without causing the world to stop you. You have no need for a broken leg.

It is generally understood that people who continually put themselves in stressful situations can develop ulcers, high blood pressure and other symptoms of *dis-ease*. Many of your traditional health practitioners are endeavoring to address these emotional and psychological causes of illness. Because of their mechanistic training, however, they are often specialized in ways that inhibit their ability to provide the care needed by multidimensional Beings —which is all of Humanity. Most efforts to treat stress related illnesses are directed toward behavior modification, a mechanistic process. Behavior modification can produce results without truly altering underlying causes, leaving a mask of health that may reveal its true face in other illnesses.

At this point in your civilization, caring for yourself as a multidimensional Being requires assembling a bevy of healers and doctors to address your wholeness. To effectively discern your course among their varying views and prescriptions adds to the stress of your health crisis—and to the growth you derive from your healing process.

The strength of the bridge between your Being and your behavior is a measure of your immediate ability to self-heal.

In *intellectually* caused illnesses any premise a person strongly believes in can lead to the override of essential instincts and the diminishing of health. If you believe you will be a more spiritual person by becoming a vegetarian, but you still crave hamburgers or pepperoni pizza, your Being is not in harmony with your behavior. If you insist upon becoming the vegetarian you think you should be, instead of the carnivore you are, you will separate yourself from yourself. At another point in your development you might make the same choice of vegetarianism, even for the same reasons, but because the choice is integral to your identity at that time you would have less craving for the foods you left behind and you would prosper rather than suffer.

Who you are on Earth right now *is* the truth of who you are on Earth. If you deny this truth, you separate from yourself and progress to your next moment without being wholly present. If you embrace who you are, you progress with presence to the next moment, ready to integrate your experience. Being present in your experience naturally facilitates you to become more fully realized tomorrow than you are today.

The way you *collectively* separate from yourselves has become a broader problem due to your current environmental conditions. Most inorganically produced foodstuffs are not of the same nature as yourselves. While inorganically produced or highly processed foods sustain you, they starve essential subtle dimensions of your well-being. When they go into your body, they are *in* you but not *of* you—because they are not *sympathetic* with your nature. This is an adversarial relationship. Who will suffer?

As you expand into higher levels of love, consciousness, integrity and response ability, you have more need to feed yourself at those levels. The more subtle vibratory elements of frequency amplitude, aroma, texture, color and integral atomic structure are absent from most manipulated, mass produced food. If you are committed to cultivating your subtle levels of awareness and you are not handling and eating foodstuffs that are alive with those vibrational frequencies and amplitudes, you are committed to a state of consciousness that you are not nourishing.

Everything you eat becomes your fingernails, your eyelashes, your hair, your skin cells, your organs and your awareness. You want your body to vibrate at the same level as the essential Universe— not the same level as the grocery store. The vibrant life frequencies and Earth nutrients provided by a delicate fresh-picked lettuce or a fresh-squeezed orange are exactly what your subtle senses need for nourishment. If these foods are not consumed immediately their subtle energy patterns (frequencies) stop generating and diminish in amplitude. The pristine sensitivities which require such immediate consumption are just what your developing awareness needs, but they are rejected as impractical for commerce.

An apple engineered to include only those characteristics that satisfy market criteria does not provide the same nourishment as an apple made up of the integral balance of all nature. Since your civilization does not yet comprehend the value of this integral balance, your technology does not test for its presence. This is understandable. You test for what you know and what you value. If the apple is tasty, attractive and nutritious to the level of your awareness, it is accepted as food for life. With undeveloped awareness you cultivate and consume food that is not sufficiently developed in its integrity to fulfill your potential for health.

Every time you permit the expulsion of waste materials into your environment you are separating from yourselves. You cannot live healthfully while inhaling these chemicals and gases, many of which are poisons. Your environment will surround and penetrate you. It will be in you, but not of you. This is an adversarial relationship. Who will suffer? Spoiling the environment is synonymous with spoiling your bodies. The two are entirely integral.

If you invent products that are not the product of your integrity, you diminish your integrity by indulging your will. Further, you *dis-integrate* many of the exquisite subtle balances of nature that produce and sustain your well-being. Until you realign these imbalances and recognize the integral nature of your worldly environment and the personal environment of your body, you will foster stress and sickness instead of well-being.

Those who manifest illness or disease are not necessarily those who participate in self-consumptive behaviors. After generations of eating and breathing combinations of chemicals that are not organic to your nature, you have begun to produce a genetic legacy that burdens the tolerances of biological nature. It is true that Human Beings are capable of profound adaptability. It is because of this adaptability that only some bodies have radiation, lead or other chemical poisoning, and only some bodies contract cancer or immune deficiency diseases.

Those who defer from making choices have increased vulnerability to illness and disease. Because their energy bonding patterns are not already organized by the glue of choice, they easily internalize things that impact their body of consciousness. Any choice you make organizes your energy toward fulfillment of that choice. Whether it is a choice of great wisdom or a shortsighted choice that will ultimately bring its measure of wisdom, a choice is an organizing principle. Until it is expanded or replaced with another choice, it will admit into the body of consciousness only that which supports its realization. This is a demonstration of Sympathetic Vibrational Magnetism.

Any misalignment with nature that extends beyond your organic tolerances will increase your vulnerability. If you are misaligned emotionally you may suffer only emotionally, but you may also suffer in your bodily health, intellectual clarity, psychological stability, transpersonal receptivity and spiritual integrity. The determinants of impact include your intentions, belief system, genetic inheritance, habituated energy patterns, and the multiple relationships of these factors.

A misalignment is the same as a misconceived or rejected value. Once a misaligned value is circulating through the consciousness of your planet, it is also circulating through the Human body. The Earth is another form of the collective Human identity. Your body and the Earth are two expressions of the same intricate formula of nature. They are both environments. Pollute one and the other is invariably polluted. If either is polluted beyond its tolerances, both will eventually demonstrate the misalignment as unwellness, disease or other forms of disintegration.

Like a Human body when its stresses exceed its tolerances and the body begins to consume itself, a planetary civilization can push beyond its biological tolerances and bring itself to an end. Just as the nucleus of a cell cannot be reconstructed or replaced, the nucleus of a civilization, if *dis-integrated*, cannot be reconstructed or replaced. It is imperative that you make choices today that preserve your privilege to make choices in the future.

Why do people get sick, have diseases and experience pain?

Is there validity to predictions
of catastrophic changes
to the Earth?

*M*Y EARTHLY BODY is born of the same elements as the Earth and comprised of the same percentages of water and minerals as is the Earth. My insight on the matter of Earth changes has as much to do with what my body tells me as with what my Universal knowledge affords me.

In this life experience on Earth I am a woman. I know the body of the Earth through my womanhood. I cycle with her moons and tides. I bear her future generations in her rhythms, by her design. I am not in a position superior to a man for this knowing; I am in a different position. Both genders are indigenous to the Earth and wholly include her nature. As a man in current civilization I would know the Earth through her forces; as a woman, through her capacities. As a man I would better know the strength of Earth's will; as a woman, her strength of willingness. The more I become aligned with my Soul resources, the more the qualities associated with each gender become embodied by the other.

When I look at the sensual curves of rolling hills and shaded valleys I see my body there, stretched out on my side like the elongated mounds and crevices of the horizon. In the outline of a single mountain I see the crook of my elbow and in another, the jutting angle of my hip bone. When the sun slips down into a sliver against the ocean I feel my breath leave my body in a slow sweet sigh. When it is gone I stand breathless, my reality merging with the invisible octaves its warmth has joined. In the morning, new life is breathed into me with an irrepressible gasp at the glory of sunrise. Surely I am the Earth changing. Surely it does not —cannot—change without me. We are one body, the Earth and me. Its changes are mine.

Does this planet Earth erupt, quake and drown its chaos any more or less than her people do? Can a multitude of people generate deep work at their core of origin, undergoing upheaval and reorganization, without the Earth—their context of embodiment— rumbling and shaking to spew out its dross and resettle in true identity?

Of course the Earth is changing with intensity—*you* are changing with intensity. Collectively you have come to the end of your capacity for denial and avoidance of your internal disruption. You can no longer maintain the schism between your Being and your behavior. You have all but consumed yourselves in trying to maintain this separation. You are ready for a new ground of being, one that unifies your heartfelt values with your actions.

Will the Earth break into pieces, condemning cities to destruction and sending countries tumbling into the sea? Will the economy collapse, returning you to a simpler life? If you cannot make changes personally you may bring them upon yourselves collectively, *forcing* the transformations you could not personally *allow*. That which you allow has the integrity and the grace of inclusion.

Rather than die, the old can transform into the new. Transformation would be better for everyone, but transforming is much harder than dying. Death takes over even where there is resistance. You can deny and fight all the way to the finish line, never having to confront yourself, never having to meet the challenge to transform. It takes far greater courage, trust, love and intelligence to reincarnate without a death. You are being asked to do this. Your cities and nations, whose disruptions of integrity and community are reflected in the Earth's breaks and upheavals, are being called upon to do this. Your economic systems and the values they derive from are being called upon to do this. Their challenge is to regenerate without death. The opportunity at hand is more than a call for transformation. It is a Universe empowered opportunity for *transmutation*, a phenomenon of grace that will swell from the transformational movement.

Who will be the first to break the momentum of the old way? Those coveting power and manipulating the economy to their ends? Those professing to hold spiritual or intellectual domain, implicitly limiting direct knowledge and exploration? Those selling toxic products? Those counseling others in the many therapies that teach people to negotiate, adapt for success and compromise, rather than to seek and follow their own inner-direction?

Who will break the momentum by jumping off the wheel of convention? How many will it take? Only one person can break the momentum—only *you*. Only you can free yourself from vested interests and learned positions, to live as you feel. Only you can invent your future integrity. In changing yourself you create a fertile environment within which others can grow and change.

Those who succeed in aligning their heartfelt values with their actions are way-makers, bridge builders to an integral way of life. Everyone who crosses the bridge makes it easier for the next person. If you are not a way-maker or an inventor, you can wait for others to offer models and means. Way-maker or follower: neither role in the collective change is greater or lesser. Pretense and competition only slow the process. Each of you is needed to be exactly what you are.

You know what needs to be done. Create new systems for sustaining your lives, founding these systems on integralism, fairness, honesty, artfulness, compassion and dedication to Universal values. Develop highly functional sources and systems for securing clean, healthy, organically produced food. Develop resources for educating children and all people to the knowledge within them, facilitating the unification of their Being and their behavior. Replace dogma with discovery. Raise your infants with personal attention and without grooming them for your societal dysfunction. Spend more time and have more pleasure with the ones you love, at the same time being independent from them in your thinking, action and exploration. Cultivate multidimensional resources for healing yourselves, so that you can proceed with personal health and well-being.

You *can* do all these things. They will establish an environment for transmutation and enable your transformational process to occur with the least amount of social chaos and personal pain. These things have not been done before because too few people had come to realize that the governing paradigm, with its competitive social systems and mechanistic conceptual systems, is arbitrary and self-limiting. You did not yet have the collective momentum to tap the powerhouse of energy that becomes available when you are a Universally aligned collective. Now that the time is right, a network of effective visionary cooperatives can activate a huge unorganized population that is ready and waiting for new models. Ask yourself how many people you know who would leap to higher ground, even at personal cost, given an effective working model? Seeing the energy amassed toward this end, we in the Greater Universe know it is already coming to pass.

In 1996 the results of a survey done in 1994 became available to the public. Sponsored by the Institute of Noetic Sciences and the Fetzer Institute, the survey conservatively estimates the size of the transformational population and identifies many of its shared values and concerns.

Characterizing those who represent transformational values as "Cultural Creatives," the survey estimates there to be 44 million Cultural Creatives in America alone. This study is a landmark within your context. It gives the transformational population a powerful position in the world's marketplace from which to influence the current, dominant material reality toward integralism—if these individuals bond and initiate collective action. Most importantly, if this study stimulates the transformational population to identify themselves as a collective and explore their influence, your planetary trans- formation can gain critical momentum.

Regardless of their faith or trust, those who break their identification with the old ways before a new world is assured face difficult issues. How will they sustain themselves? How will their needs be met? How will they align with others of like mind? How will they share their resources of imagination and practical ingenuity? It is easy to see why many choose *not* to make the changes needed to honor themselves and express the integrity of All That Is.

By working in concert, those of you who have higher understanding in your respective fields can establish leadership centers to generate the educational information needed to replace mechanistic thinking. Collectively you have the skills to design and implement the new models needed for integral social function resulting from this information. So long as these centers maintain integrity, you will have ready access to Universal Beings who have mastery in counterpart disciplines. With such resources aligned, these will become centers for Universal collaboration, training, and the dissemination and practical application of Universal knowledge.

If our invitation inspires you to participate in a Universal dialogue, advanced Universe Beings will assist you in developing practical plans for collective transformation. Your challenge is to transform the systems already in place. You do not have to dismantle your existing structures and organizations and begin anew. There is nothing wrong with these structures. What is necessary is to raise their functions to higher levels of integrity. To accomplish this all technology needs to be fully compatible and the information purveyed needs to be updated. The language can no longer be mechanistic, competitive and centered in economics. All mechanistic information is already outdated. Competition is making you better at what does not work. And the economy is a completely illusory value system—even in its own context. The new language derives from energy, integralism, love and compassion. The tools you need are currently in development in your society. Some are already available for application. Some are temporarily thwarted from application by vested interests and established momentum.

Many of you think you need to be more than you are now before you can make a contribution that will change the world. This is not so. Each of you has enlightenment in your life. Focus yourself in these places where your enlightenment is found. This is your most fertile ground for growth and contribution. All that is unresolved or unknown within you will eventually appear where you stand with enlightenment, because it yearns to a become part of that sacred ground of being.

The belief that one person cannot change the course of the world is held by enough people to touch hands all the way around the Earth. You are not only a person. You are also a frequency and a value that permeates the Universe. When the choices you make in your daily life and the quality of love you demonstrate in your daily life are consistent with your essential nature, your actions impact more than you knowingly touch. They impact the movement of All That Is. Most people do not believe they are this important because they do not perceive themselves as essential participants in the Greater Universe.

You only experience that which you include. What you do not include happens anyway, outside of your awareness. If you think of yourself as a city person, you will experience the city communicating with you. If you think of yourself as a northerner, you will identify with all that is northern. If you think of yourself as an Earthling, you will sense the Earth. And if you think of yourself as part of the Universe, your experience will embrace the Universal. The locus of belonging you identify with becomes your medium for feedback and growth.

In any process there are moments of doing and moments of being. If you cannot see what you can do to contribute, rest assured that your way of being in the world has equal impact. It is a rotational kind of task, the transformation of reality. Each time the Earth moves around the sun the collective awakens yet again. Each day calls for some to do and some to be. Your tasks will become clear to you when their moments arise. Like the sandbagging of a dam during a flood, everyone's participation is needed to pass the bags. There is no thought of whose hands they pass through first or last, or of what place one has in the line. Those who lend their boots to those who work the line are equal in participation. Do not try to measure your value in this change by education, wealth or leadership capacity. Your value is intrinsic. Your presence to the change makes the change.

Each time you expand, include, and integrate something you formerly held to be outside of your love or beyond your capacity, you are bringing the world closer to its opportunity for transmutation. Each time you express your highest truth and support others in expressing theirs, you are moving the world. All the plans and all the dollars in the world cannot do this. This job belongs to each and serves all. It is the claiming of personal integrity. There are none better or less equipped—it is only that some are more practiced.

Live as if the world were already as you wish it would be and it will be so.

*Why is it so hard for people
to realize their dreams?*

REAMS ARE AS REAL AS YOU ARE—and as changeable over time. Many people share in the struggle to realize their dreams in the world. They are able to envision and work for their dreams, yet they cannot seem to bring them about. Often they believe that the fulfillment of their dreams requires others—sometimes everyone else—to change. Those of you who feel this way are poised at the threshold of a unique opportunity to test your hypothesis. The opening of the new millennium promises to be an epoch of phenomenal individual and planetary change.

The best way to realize your dreams is to live to the fullest the moment you are in. Each moment will bring before you your next opportunity for dream fulfillment. If what the moment offers you does not look like your dream, it is an opportunity for growth that is prerequisite to your dream.

Suppose you wish to meet the man or woman of your dreams. You may even call on the Universe, asking us to help you bring that person into your life. There is no reason why your wish should not come true. Energy wasted in longing would be far better expressed in loving. Day after day you hold onto this dream and day after day

what comes to you seems to be everything *but* your dream.
You think you must be doing something wrong, but you are not.

It would not serve you if the person of your dreams arrived in your life before you knew how to accept his or her love, and how to offer your own in successful relationship. To have a fulfilling, loving relationship you might first need to make discoveries about yourself, about communication or about the nature of relationship. Your embrace and integration of these discoveries may be prerequisite to successful realization of your dream. Making these discoveries could even redefine your dream.

The way discoveries unfold is unique to each person and each dream. Day by day, the experiences that can precipitate realization of your dream will come before you and fill the space in your life wherein you wish your dream would live. Eventually, by embracing these challenges, the opportunity that stands before you *will be your dream*. It may not appear so, but you always have before you exactly what you need. Trusting that the process is unfolding in this way enables you to perceive your dream in the process of realization.

In addition to embracing what the moment before you offers, there is another way to empower the realization of a dream. If you stand on the outside of a dream, imagining it, your magnetism for attracting what you need in order to bring that dream into reality is relatively weak. Realizing a dream from the outside is like trying to paint a huge mural of intensely colored images with an airbrush. Each time you focus your energy on your dream, a diffused spray of dream paint gets airbrushed into reality. Eventually, layer by layer, substantive images will be amassed and elements from your dream will begin to appear in your life—but an airbrush is a highly inefficient tool for the job.

Thoughts are indeed things. Thoughts and intentions are forms of magnetic stimuli to which energy responds (SVM). This response behavior of energy is fundamental to its nature, regardless of one's ethics, morality or consciousness. If you consistently put your energy into producing the images you associate with your dream, you will eventually produce those images in your life. But…your images are not necessarily the fulfillment of your dream.

It takes a lot of time and energy to create a dream from the outside with an airbrush. When it finally becomes a fully painted reality and you inhabit it, you may find that you have created what you imagined, but from the *inside* it is not what you actually want. This is often what happens when dreamers stand outside of their dreams, separate from them, creating them. Why not inhabit your dream from the start? Inhabiting your dream before you devote yourself to producing its images empowers you to realize what you are truly seeking.

To optimize your alignment for bringing a dream to realization, translate your dream from images into values and feelings, and inhabit the values and feelings of your dream.

When you visualize, contemplate or meditate on your dream, or when you are communicating your dream to others, ask yourself: "What part of myself am I seeking to express by living this dream? What aspects of myself will gain realization? What values will I have an opportunity to explore?

What will I bring to life? How will I feel living in this dream? How will I grow?"

These questions will enable you to identify the values inherent to your dream. It is these values, rather than the images you have dressed them in, that you are longing to inhabit. And it is inhabiting these values that aligns you to magnetize your dream into reality. Once you identify the values and find the feelings that will come to life in the realization of your dream, inhabit them deeply every time you visit your dream. When you inhabit these values and feelings you generate a magnetic field for dream realization that is profoundly more powerful than the field generated by visualizing your dream from an emotional distance. This is the alchemy of dream realization.

Visualization is a powerful tool not because of the images you create, but because of the values and feelings you inadvertently inhabit while constructing the thoughts or images. Things and images have only temporal and representative meaning. Values are Universal, eternal and charged with momentum for manifestation.

Identifying the values and feelings of a dream is not the hard part of performing the alchemy of dream realization. The challenge is to *inhabit* these values and feelings. Why is this difficult? To inhabit them you will have to experience your doubt, your actual distance from readiness, the depth of your desire, and your worthiness for fulfillment. You will have to embrace challenges and feelings you have not yet allowed yourself to include. If you had, your dream would already be manifest in your life.

When I was a young woman I was living in Arizona on a modest budget. Although my little two bedroom house in the middle of town was charming, I had a deep unexplainable desire to move. Imagining the place I would like to live, I saw a cottage with two bedrooms (one of them large enough for a queen size bed), a living room with a nook for my desk, a cozy kitchen with lots of sunlight and a private backyard.

I knew I wanted a quiet, cheerful place in nature with a lot of privacy and an extra room for guests. I did not know at the time that I was creating an environment where I would explore and develop my skills as a healer—a purpose best fulfilled without observers and in the rhythms of an unpeopled natural setting. It was this higher purpose and its inherent values that provided the stimuli I interpreted as a quiet place in nature—a cottage with two bedrooms (one of them large enough for a queen size bed), a living room with a nook for my desk, a cozy kitchen with lots of sunlight and a private backyard.

When I talked with friends about my dream, hoping to enlist them as rental scouts, they laughed at the notion of a cottage in the desert. What the southwestern desert had to offer was haciendas, guest houses, stuccos and ranchitos—not cottages. I decided to enlist the Universe in my search, but I was not sure where to look for the response. Did being alert to a response from the Universe mean I would have to read every posted notice in town, even the bulletin board in the laundromat? In contemplation before meditating I invited the Universe to use the newspaper as the medium for its response, and I committed myself to checking the rental listings daily.

To better connect with the Universe and my dream, in the evenings I turned on music and danced, allowing the feelings of my dream to rise in me and inspire me to claim them. After several of these evenings I began to sense emerging aspects of myself and new qualities of being, but I could not fully inhabit them. There was something in the way. I had unrecognized resistance to realizing my own dream: Would I be socially isolated if I left the heart of town? Would I feel safe living in the desert without neighbors? I thought I was being challenged to meet my doubts and fears about making a new home beyond the edge of town. Unknowingly, I was being challenged to meet my doubts and fears about making a new home beyond the edge of *common reality*. I was confronting deeper life questions: Do I have the courage to depart from my peers and our shared life style to pursue the more singular and internal path of a healer? Will I be safe exploring the edge of the unknown?

Each day for several weeks I read the newspaper rental listings morning and night, finding nothing. After a few weeks a listing appeared in the daily paper for a two-room guest cottage. Two rooms was too small and the rent was more than I thought I could afford, but on principle I had to respond to an ad for a *cottage*. I expected to satisfy my obligation to the Universe with a quick visit and continue looking for a place with two bedrooms (one large enough for a queen size bed), a living room with a nook for my desk, a cozy kitchen with lots of sunlight and a private backyard.

When I called in response to the ad the owners were very encouraging. They said I would have to see the place to fully appreciate it. Right they were! It was only two rooms, but one was a huge main room with high vega beams, a fireplace, two sets of French doors and a sunny tiled kitchen area; and the other was a small bedroom surrounded by a garden that looked onto thirty acres of untouched desert land. The ad had not mentioned the small screened porch suitable for an almost year around guest bed or work space. There I was with a bedroom only big enough for a double bed, no second bedroom, no defined backyard—and no question that it was the right place. Walking through it I felt just the way I felt when I was dancing in my living room, inhabiting my dream.

In the process of inhabiting a dream, as you approach the deep feelings and potentials that would be fulfilled in its realization, you encounter the resistance that has been keeping the dream from becoming reality. Whether the resistance is personal or collective in nature, you have to dissolve it within yourself. In order to generate the magnetism that will turn your dream into reality, you may have to reawaken the pain and disappointment you have suffered in longing for the dream and in feeling its absence. This pain and disappointment can preoccupy your will and worthiness, withholding your energy from dream realization. There is no rational way to avoid the pains of resistance. Even if you crawl slowly toward them, you must leap through them with a fierceness of deserving. The very act of leaping into the heart of your dream will transmute the energy of your resistance into creative magnetism for dream realization.

What if the resistance you meet is not your own? There might be societal limitations that restrict the fulfillment of your dream. If you dream of teaching elementary school in an enlightened environment with other like-minded teachers of both genders, while earning a living equal to your friends with mid-level corporate jobs, you will face significant societal limitations. You could have a hard time convincing yourself that it is worth believing in such an impractical dream. Yet this dream could become a reality. By enbracing the societal limitations, you can *surrender your images and seek the values*. Once you free yourself from the images, the values may present themselves in a different way to fulfill your dream. You might attract an opportunity to teach in an elementary school that serves a special interest community. The school may have more female teachers than male, but be located in a community where mothers and fathers participate equally with educators in decision-making. The freedoms offered you by the school administration may permit your classroom to be as enlightened as you are. Along with emotional riches, the closeness of the community may afford you goods, services and opportunities that significantly increase your pay. While different from your ideas and images, this opportunity provides all the values you need to fulfill your dream.

The greatest gift of inhabiting the values and feelings of a dream is that the process itself informs you of the creative power of your internal resources. You need no longer wonder *if* the dream will come to be, or *how*, or *when*. Your own inner experience reveals whatever you need to embrace in order to bring your dream into reality. While these examples have been individual in nature, world peace, environmental sanctity and Human awakening can be reached by the same means.

*Is there good and evil
in the Greater Universe?*

*C*ONSIDER A UNIVERSE REALITY that is nonjudgmental, its powers and potentials not intrinsically limited or enhanced by ideas of good and bad. How do you feel about a Universe whose potentials are not protected from use by any prerequisite standard of personal ethics or spiritual awareness? This picture of the power of the Universe is like electricity—it is equally available to those who wish to create with it and to those who wish to kill with it.

Universal integrity is fundamentally inherent to all life, making it unnecessary to protect life from itself in any of its infinite manifestations.

There is no such thing as bad energy. All ideas of good and bad, or good and evil, are local to the dualistic environments within which they are conceived. Negative ideas and the behaviors they spawn reflect inverted or misaligned values. They do not derive from something "other than" or competitive with Universal values.

What if the "negative" in a person's consciousness is just their unconsciousness waiting to become empowered by essential stimuli and directed toward Universal potentials? What if there is no independent force of negativity or evil? Inversion, misalignment and unconsciousness are within the tolerances of the Universe and embraced within Universal love. Do the actions that violate you hurt any less if you call them bad or evil? Their instances may be diminished by laws of deterrence and punishments that derive from social ideas of good and bad, but the violations spring from ignorance or developmental damage, not from evil.

―――――――――――――― ∽◦∾ ――――――――――――――

Negative energy *is energy that is not yet expressive of its Universal nature and not yet directed toward its Universal potentials.*

Positive energy *is energy that is expressive of its Universal nature and directed toward its Universal potentials.*

Nothing essential to Universal reality is dualistic. What may be judged by those on Earth to be a negative force, is seen by Universe Beings as energy or consciousness that is not yet informed of its integrity with All That Is. When energy and the consciousness that magnetizes it produce forces that diminish integrity and love in the world, they are expressing their ignorance. Negative consciousness is ignorant—willfully or innocently—of Universal values. Whether it is denied or acknowledged, those who perpetuate negativity live in fear and pain.

―――――――――――――― ∽◦∾ ――――――――――――――

Where Universal values are not demonstrating integrity, they will be demonstrating misalignment or inversion. There really is nothing else to manifest. Whether they are rightside up, upside down or sideways, Universal values, in their infinite relationships and unrevealed potentials, are all there is in the Universe. Ideas founded upon inverted or misconceived values produce what you experience as *bad*—whether these ideas arise from you as the perceiver or are actually expressed in what you are perceiving. While you may attribute the bad to some purposefully evil force, your devils are not actual identities who cause trouble. They are your personification of the collective trouble you produce through innocence and ignorance. With this understanding, instead of blaming or diminishing yourself and others when you encounter negativity, you can embrace it as a space within the infinite relationships of being, where Universal values are not yet aligned.

Even in extreme cases of human destructiveness this principle holds true. Those who "belong to" gangs and commit gang violence are not evil. While their means and context are misconceived, they are putting everything on the line in order to experience a Universal value: unity. Their behavior says, "We don't belong anywhere." Their behavior also says, "We are seeking something that will give life value: spiritual bonds and committed family relationships that protect our members unconditionally." Since protection, devotion, reliability and unconditional love are not forthcoming from their daily world, gang leaders are attempting to legislate and enforce these Universal values relative to their context. Is this really any different from a government legislating or enforcing the Universal value of equality, regardless of belief or color? Both groups govern

through control and punishment. The difference is in the accepta-
bility of their means. Isn't it just a matter of which gang you are in?

To accurately identify the path toward world peace and integrity
you must be able to hear the common call for Universal values.
It is necessary to recognize and appreciate the energy of these
values in whatever forms they may appear. When these values
emerge naturally from dysfunction, prize them even in their states
of misconception. Those who imbue personal chaos with values
have unknowingly dropped a taproot in the ground of integrity.
Grow them where they are planted until the season is ripe for
rerouting them into greater light.

Being able to recognize the intentions behind crooked or odd applications of values helps you see how to straighten them out. If you
call these ignorant demonstrations *evil*, the instinctive responses
are to stamp them out or to keep away from them. However, if you
recognize them as misconceptions based on the absence of higher
understanding, the natural response is to engage and to provide
what is needed. This inclusion initiates the remedy.

When you are the one who is suffering because of others' acts of
ignorance, no measure of understanding and inclusion can undo the
circumstances. What understanding and inclusion *can* do is provide
a regenerative context in which to heal your suffering.

Everyone is always doing the best they can—not the best they can
imagine—but the best they can actually demonstrate from where
they are, where they have been and what they understand about
life and love. It is shortsighted to judge those who are offensive or
ignorant as somehow *other* than yourself. Their ignorance is just
more obvious, ugly, illegal or socially unacceptable than yours.

Judgments of good and bad do not exist among Universal Beings. Conditions you might call positive and negative do exist, but within a continuum, not in opposition to one another. They exist as points on a spiral that naturally elevates toward integrity. When you watch a feature film in a movie theater you focus on the characters and the developing story. You do not focus on the content of each frame as if it were a still photograph. If you were to freeze each frame of dialogue from a well-polished film there would be many images of the hero and heroine with their tongues sticking out, their eyes crossed and other facial contortions. These could be considered negative or bad images. Looking at these frames out of the context of their cinematic continuum, you might conclude that the film is bad and not worth including in your experience.

Universal Beings effortlessly see the continuum. This is something most Human Beings do not yet know how to do. To know where to look for the bigger picture and how to see it, Humanity will have to answer many questions about the nature of reality. What is a life? Where can its purpose be found? What is fulfillment? What is the relationship of the individual to the collective? To discover answers to these questions two things need be done: begin to entertain the meaning and the option of a nondualistic reality; and endeavor to look at yourself and others through the lens of unconditional love.

Liberation from dualism brings the understanding that there is no inherently destructive force. There is only energy, in endless configurations, constantly moving through varying conditions of ignorance and enlightenment, toward self-realization and Universal integrity.

Unconditional love means there are no conditions to diminish the constancy and quality of your love. It does not mean there are no requirements for relationship and no critical or discerning freedoms. Unconditional love includes criticism, dissatisfaction, anger and disappointment, and can express them honestly without projecting blame. The Human understanding of unconditional love often confuses discernment with making judgments and assigning blame. To expect yourself or others to love without discernment is unnatural. Discernment is a fundamental characteristic of consciousness. It grows in each of us as we grow toward greater enlightenment. You need not make or pass a judgment; every action reveals its own. Judgment is inherent in the quality of every action, behavior and demonstration of every Being. The judgment derives from how far the intention and action are from their initiator's capacity for integrity at that moment. It is not a subjective critical assessment.

This description of judgment is consistent with the idea of sin. Sin was historically defined as "missing the mark," not as a personal failure or a violation of God. Humanity's understanding of both unconditional love and sin became misaligned in the confusion of making judgments. Judgment is observed in relation to potential. It is not blameful. Of course, no one can control the way another person receives reflection or feedback. People who do not experience unconditional love, because they feel unworthy of it or have suffered damage to their internal authority, most often experience feedback as judgmental and blameful.

Unconditional love is the bridge that will elevate you above the dualism of good and bad. Living with this inclusive heartfulness frees you from emotional entanglement, leaving your energy available to facilite resolutions and unifications in yourself and in your world.

Do we in the Cosmos
have relationships
and fall in love?

WE IN THE COSMOS do fall in love. We fall in love in order to get *into* our dimensions—like Alice down the rabbit hole. Falling into the *state of being love* is not about loving another person. It is about loving everything —All That Is.

In the dimensions of my current Cosmic experience, because we are already in the state of being love when we are drawn to one another, we cannot help but be in love with every Being with whom we enter into relationship. Still, in each intimate relationship we experience alignments and intensities of feeling that are unique to that union. Sometimes what we in the Cosmos feel and how we express ourselves resembles what you feel and express when you fall in love. However, even when our responses are like yours they will not have your meanings and implications. We in the Greater Universe do not construct meanings and implications. We have direct experience and direct expansion. Our experience is direct because we have no subconscious/conscious separation. Holding aspects of reality apart from your direct experience requires you to have a separation between your subconscious and conscious awareness. There is nothing we feel the need to withhold from ourselves, individually or collectively. There is no experience or perception we want to exclude. Being fully integrated, we have nothing to reconcile from the past. We are current with our reality and trust it to reveal the expanding nature of All That Is.

Space/time being an option rather than a constant, it is nearly impossible for us to become contained by any relationship. Our axial value and our multidimensionality assure that we will each continue to experience dimensions of personal and Universal reality beyond those aligned between us. Because we do not maintain a time continuum, a present moment does not necessarily define a future moment. This means love shared between Beings in a relationship does not lead to any established behaviors or actions. We do not move in together. There are no engagements, marriages or divorces. Our nature does not preclude lifelong relationships; it supports them. There is, however, no status or value afforded to them that is not afforded to all relationships. Our shared love can produce combinations of identity and value that activate new possibilities in each of us. This activation might even empower a new energy constellation—the birth of a new frequency/value or a new combinant frequency/value, in the form of offspring.

The biggest difference between Universal lovers and Human lovers is that we in the Cosmos approach intimacy to discover what lives in the moment if we don't put anything there. We do not replace the essence of the moment with what we wish would be there or with what has been there in a past moment.

What attracts any one Being to any other is more subtle and multidimensional than can be readily imagined. Beyond the apparent connection there is a unique and invisible alignment of variables. Even though you may feel them, on Earth you usually do not recognize the invisible dimensions that are attracting you to one another. Often, before you allow yourselves enough time to fully inhabit these unique alignments, you limit their potential by launching into a familiar or desired form of relationship.

This is common between lovers. As soon as your attraction is mutually acknowledged, your projections are unleashed and the multidimensional potentials recede from consciousness. Your projections quickly become the axis of the affection you have for one another. If they override the actual identity and the expressed values of the other person, you isolate yourself from the experience of relationship. You may think you are wrapping your arms around the other person, but you are really wrapping your arms around your own projections. What gives a new relationship such immediate depth and/or momentum is the Universal energy of alignment that brought you together. What makes physical affection feel so genuine so quickly—when it is unlikely you know each other well enough to elicit it—is your intimate familiarity with your own projections.

Empowered by the momentum of projection you can become deeply engaged in real feelings that are fueled by your imagination, and be pained by the result of your own invention. It is difficult to be on either side of that experience—the person inventing the illusion or the person being invented. It is not difficult to understand how you become an illusionmaker when you really yearn to be a lover. It is the displacement of a profound *spiritual* drive: In an attempt to satisfy your desire for unification within your own

Being, you merge with others upon whom you have projected the constructions that would resolve your own feelings of incompleteness and separation.

If you are relating to the potential self of someone who is not devoted to manifesting that self, you are loving a person who is not really there. Loving another person's potential instead of what is actual will not produce the equality that nourishes a love relationship. Eventually you will get angry and hurt because the person you love and believe in so deeply is not there for you. In fact, that person never was there for you— except in your projection. At the same time, the other person will begin to feel that you are not satisfied, not really there, not appreciative or not really in love with them. All these things are true. You are tolerating the person your loved one actually is, while waiting for your vision of your loved one to show up.

You do not have to be free of the Earth to be free of these entrapments. You need only love others for who they are and build your relationships upon what is actual rather than what is possible. This means recognizing and supporting whichever values are being expressed through the personalities and behaviors of those you love. If potential is ready to emerge, it will emerge in this supportive environment. Asking people to manifest values that are not being generated from within them will at best produce behavioral changes. Integral development requires integral motivation. Most people assume that loving the potential within another person will bring it forth, eventually making it possible to have the other's potential self as your loved one. This is only true when the other person is initiating the self-development. One who does not initiate self-realization will not have the resources to sustain it. Your love is essential as support, but you cannot produce another's awakened self. All are entitled to discover and bring forth their potential self in their own timing.

People who are separated from the aspiration to express Universal values usually behave according to their past conditioning, rather than their essential nature. They behave from *reaction* more often than from conscious *response*. When integrity is not the motivating force for growth, people change to win success rather than to gain self-realization.

Our Cosmic reality system is not founded on the same organization of values as yours and our lives are not founded on the same ideas as yours. Our relationships, therefore, are not like yours. We do not need reasons for our actions. We act because we are so moved, because it feels right and because it expresses us. It is unusual for any one of us to ask what others are doing or why they are doing it. The *what* is obvious. All are capable of perceiving it. The *why* is often so multidimensional that to fully communicate it would require explaining the whole of one's personal reality. Then the *why* would make perfect and obvious sense. Since appreciation of this is a given in our reality, we do not seek explanations. Our individual and collective integrity enables us to live in our experience without need for content analysis. Everything is precisely what it is. We are not distanced from our knowledge by things *seeming* to be or pretending to be.

Since we already know that every Being has integrity and the actions of every Being are integral, we do not need to study or evaluate each other to develop trust and understanding. Each of us is self-directed with such integrity that we do not consider or critique one another's choices unless we are collaborating in discovery. When we have an agreement to collaborate, our feedback to one another is uninhibited by the need for tact or by concerns of vulnerability. Being current and having nothing to hide makes vulnerability our natural state. In fact, our vulnerability permits us to be perpetually receptive to information. We are always semi-permeable. We respond to whatever impresses us by growing to include it. We are constantly informing, enriching and inspiring each other, but we do not address ourselves to the process by which this occurs. We are sufficiently secure in ourselves and our trust of one another to live without keeping track of our relationships in a linear or analytical fashion. This affords us great emotional and creative freedom.

If we wish to know the intimate content that resulted in another's expression we need only invite that Being into a *merge,* a glorious experience of mental, emotional and sensual union. This is one of the many forms of making love in our dimension. When we merge with another Being's personal reality, our mutual intention determines the level of our experience. We can watch the content of the other Being's life; we can conceptually know it; we can feel it; or we can fully experience it as if we were living it. At this most complex level, we so become the Being with whom we have merged that we experience exactly as that Being experiences, retaining no independent point of view. Only when we return to our own identity at the completion of the merge does the other Being's content take on the quality of relativity.

Many sensitive people in your society are beginning to experience their capacity for this type of merging. Their natural development of this ability implies that they have the discernment necessary to surrender and reclaim their individuation. These people are generating a magnetic field that stimulates more of you to actualize your potential for merging.

In addition to this natural expansion, you have a large population of people who, as a result of injured childhood development, have been unknowingly merging with others throughout their lives. The injury sustained by these people is contained within the dynamics of your local, temporal reality. The healthful identity of each of them is preserved and accessible at the Universal, or Soul, level. By learning to convert the sloppy boundaries of unintentional merging, into the graceful bridges of conscious merging, these individuals can access the healing resources of their Souls. In their processes of self-healing they can reinstate personal well-being and provide healing stimuli for the Human collective.

Unfortunately, there are few among your therapeutic community who recognize this opportunity. Many of those who counsel see merging as a loss of boundaries—an undesirable thing, rather than a transcendence of boundaries—a Universal resource. As a client in the therapeutic process one is asked to examine foundations. When foundations are put into question there is often little or no healthy ground left to stand on. For those who relate intimately to others by merging, it is devastating to be asked to eliminate that mode of relating and give up their ground of intimacy. A skyhook such as the ability to merge with others, can be a healing resource and an empowerment when one's foundation is in question.

Although entering and exiting a merge cleanly takes some practice, one can learn to discern when a merge is occurring. If a therapist learns how to direct the merge capacity toward the Soul, the client will locate an innate healer and self-worth will sprout from a new and sacred ground of being. Once self-worth is refounded, the healing of past experience generates spontaneously (SVM) and supports the work of the therapist. This is therapeutic alchemy.

The capacity to transcend boundaries provides all people with an exceptional opportunity to experience as another person experiences. In defining boundaries as a means of protection and of keeping things out, your current culture has popularized a misconception. By making choices in truthful response to your nature, boundaries are naturally produced around what you include...until you grow to include All That Is and boundaries become meaningless.

The door to the rabbit hole is open. We look forward to falling into love with you.

How can Humanity
free its children from
the patterns of the past?

*T*O FREE YOUR CHILDREN from the limiting Human patterns of the past, help them stay aligned with Universal values. Integrity, compassion and creativity are an excellent start on life. Love the children unconditionally and abundantly. Do not hurry them into worldly rhythms or busy them with materialism and excessive activity. Encourage each child's unique value to manifest without imposing developmental expectations on their early years.

You have recently discovered that little ones have extra-ordinary learning capacities. This is true. Why busy these exceptional capacities with the unexceptional content of academic learning? Traditional education is integral to your civilization and will become a part of their knowledge in ample time for meaningful use. Your children's early capacities for learning are profound precisely because they precede the imposition of worldly constructs of intelligence. Until these resources are entrained by worldly patterns or directed elsewhere, they enable each child to continue to adjust his or her frequency/value for self-realization in the world by engaging with multidimensional stimuli that worldly

minds rarely perceive. Why harness the profound potentials
of an infant or preschooler and address them to the mundane?
The profound learning capacities of prenatal and preschool
children are not needed for these ends. Those children who
are drawn to reading, mathematics or languages in their
first years will let you know they want these stimuli and will
practice these skills as play.

Current research tells you that brain patterns change and extra-ordinary learning potentials narrow as children reach ages three and four. These first years are considered to be a biological window of opportunity. The research tells you how these potentials narrow, but not why. The narrowing occurs because the children begin accommodating to the limited local stimuli and amplitudes being offered them. By age three or four the multidimensional conscious-ness of a child has no integral place in the world. It is isolated to creative play and fantasy, receiving little or no reinforcement or stimulation from intimate fellows—parents, family, community. Unsuccessful at communicating with the world in their primary nonverbal language of vibrational stimuli and responses, children adapt for the native tongue and begin to perform within the local constructs of intelligence.

You would enlighten the future of Humanity dramatically if you could keep the dysfunction of the world from intruding into the consciousness of your children until they have reached the age of seven. Even if you can only preserve their primary state until age four, it will have an enlightening impact on the future of the world. Trying to prepare preschool children for the world by exposing them to "realistic" stories is not a service to them. Trying to enlist young children in righting the wrongs of the world is not a service to them. There are better mediums for their personal and social empowerment.

Rather than giving young children an outlet for their fears and pains about the world, premature exposure to life's cruelties, as in Grimm's Fairy Tales, introduces and reinforces the fears and dysfunctions of the world. Philosophers and psychologists who have said otherwise may have been viewing identity as stemming from a humanized psyche rather than a Universal Soul. Even your most Universally attuned educational philosophies purvey fairy tales of inhumanity, manipulation and violence, believing them to empower the children through identification with characters who meet and overcome travail. If this were the case, why would so many children have bad dreams and fears after exposure to Hansel and Gretel, Little Red Riding Hood and like tales? When these exposures come too early they pull a child into worldly dualism, setting up internal coping and desensitization mechanisms that distance the child from his or her own internal blueprint for a loving and integral life. It is the children and their internal blueprints that hold the stimuli for your planetary healing. You do not want to bury these maps before the children can read them.

———————— ✎ ————————

The self-limiting conditions Humanity currently lives within are essentially transitory, but they have been so long habitu- ated into Human behavior that they have become intrinsic to Human embodiment. Even in the best situations children are rarely born into the world without veils of limiting collective heredity. By the time of birth the emotional and psychological body of each infant holds the habituated patterns of the collective, sorted by familial magnetism into latent or dominant characteristics. In the first four to seven years a child's environment and experience can reorganize the dominance and latency patterns of both familial and collective characteristics.

In infancy and early childhood inherited behavioral constructions are malleable and patterning can be liberated from these configurations. Most children, however, are raised by those who have genetically transmitted these emotional and psychological habits to them. If parents have not acknowledged and healed these patterns in themselves, their children usually remain entrained by the parental behavior. Entrainment, of course, can occur with the family's strengths as well as its self-limiting patterns. When people do heal their own self-limiting patterns, it takes four to seven years for cellular regeneration to form a whole cellular body that is patterned in the healed condition. If a child is conceived after the body has generated cellular integrity in the healed condition, the self-limiting pattern will *not* pass on to offspring as dominant.

Ideally, children's caregivers and social experience would be free of dualistic and other self-limiting stimuli, causing these collective habit patterns to recede into eventual extinction. In most instances however, the behavioral stimuli established prenatally and in the first four years of life shape a child's life-long dominant and latent behavior patterns. The more Universally attuned a child's familial and environmental stimuli, the longer this shaping period can extend. Shaping of behavioral dominances and latencies can occur all the way to age seven in children who have not been overly directed and defined nor conformed to societal dysfunction.

The familial behavior patterns passed on to children come from both parents and begin forming in the offspring at the moment of conception. The father is not the passive participant he is currently believed to be. He is modeling and influencing the behavioral characteristics of his offspring from the moment of conception, regardless of his physical proximity or level of interaction with the mother and baby.

If those who are raising a child know how to recognize self-limiting behaviors when they first demonstrate in infancy and early childhood, with conscious attention they can liberate their child from the dominance of these patterns. When working to liberate genetic behavioral patterns the child's interpersonal stimuli are critical. This is when a child needs the most personal and unique forms of loving attention. As the provider of this attention you need to be free from models and expectations of what you or your child should be doing or looking like to others.

Eating problems are a common example of individual behavior that results from collective hereditary patterning. When parents and primary caregivers reject rather than nurture a child, a reactive behavioral pattern is established in relation to nurturance. After generations of these stimuli and their reactions, a collective Human heredity pattern has been established that may become manifest in *any* child as an eating disturbance.

Wee ones need to experience nurturance as coming from within —from within themselves, from within their caregivers and from within the rhythms of Human life. When infants are breastfed (or if breastfeeding is not possible, bottlefed) they need to be embraced at your chest to feel your heartbeat. It attunes them to the rhythms of Human beingness and Human nurturance. Putting a wee one with a bottle into a crib, playpen or stroller, externalizes the locus of nurturance. Instead of placing it within the rhythms and feelings of embodiment, it displaces nurturance to external contexts. If an infant is not breastfed or held at the heart until he or she is ready to stop feeding, you may reinforce an inherited nurturance rejection pattern or stimulate its behavioral component. This could result in eating problems or emotional disturbances in relation to eating or drinking. If these behaviors demonstrate, you may have to hold your infant or toddler lovingly on your lap at mealtimes for a year or two—without forcing food consumption— before a genetically conveyed rejection of nurturance will be healed.

As Earth's planetary transformation progresses toward transmutation, the lower amplitude levels that hold your local dysfunctional patterns will be generously overwhelmed by a spectrum of higher amplitudes. Fortunately, the material level of a child is their most temporal level. While genetic history strongly influences behavior, it is but a scrim to the Being incarnating as a child. The frequency/ value of that Being and the purposes of incarnation are profoundly more essential to the nature of the Being and will emerge and gain dominance when allowed.

Were it not for the children and the enthusiasm they bring for invisible reality, fewer adults on your planet would entertain *the unseen* and *the not yet realized*. The beauty emanating from children in those moments when the invisible fills their eyes with responsive radiance and plumps their skin to bursting, has always been cherished among you. It rekindles in grown ones a desire to make the world a place where children's dreams could come true. It reminds the grown ones, if only for a fleeting moment, that they have made tacit agreements to ignore their dreams and conform to established notions of what is real and important.

Generations of Human Beings who have closed the doors to magic in their own lives continue to read and tell magical stories to their children. It is one of the most commonly shared experiences in the development of children on your planet. There are few values that are so inclusively and cross-culturally sustained in child rearing. It is clear that you believe the magical potentials of the Universe are important. In this you have great wisdom.

Unfortunately, there comes a time in your parenting of children when you feel you must ready them for reality as you know it. In your fear that magical thinking will inhibit their practical development, cause them disappointment or result in their inability to adapt to a lesser beauty, you train them to trade multidimensionality for the mundane. This assures a mundane future for your world.

This cycle of self-limitation will repeat until there comes a generation of parents who do not sell lost hope to their children, but instead reclaim the magical stories and find the courage to make them real. Until that happens, the children and a scattered population of inspired people who hold the magic beans, are preserving the wonders and possibilities of the magical world. They are holding the ground that will yield abundantly in this transformative cycle of Humanity.

Is it possible
  for all of Humanity
    to share a common vision?

*I*T IS MORE THAN theoretically possible for Humanity to share a common vision. You have already done it. Your planet Earth could not have come to be unless all those who formulated its reality shared a common vision at its point of conception.

A reality system is born when a collective of Beings shares a conception of Universal values that has no existing environment for its realization.

When there is no "place" to realize a collective vision, the collective and the vision can create a place. The energy and/or mass needed to produce their desired context will naturally accumulate through the processes of alignment and merging that constitute the dynamics of creation. The context that is collectively created could be a planet, a star, or a new dimension of an existing planet or star. The phenomenon of creating a context from a merge of collective resources is no different and no more or less divine than the phenomenon of creating a child from the merge of bodily resources.

Each reality context in the Universe expresses all frequencies and values, but in differing patterns of alignment and relationship than any other. The axial frequencies and values of the Beings who conceive a context are intrinsically central to their created context. All other frequencies and values will constellate around these initiating values, in patterns that ultimately express the nature of that context. This is what causes the environment—the "Mother Nature" of each context—to be unique. Trees, rivers, minerals, gases, animals and sea life are some of the manifestations that occurred when planet Earth was patterned from a collective intention.

Once a collective produces an environment to embody its conception, the participants in the collective need to be able to inhabit their environment as individual identities. The bodies and forms they create in order to inhabit their context will express the same configuration of frequencies and values that characterize their context. The forms follow the function of the context.

The context of a reality system reflects the collective identity of its creators, focused toward a common purpose.

The content of a reality system reflects the identities that formed the collective and their freedom as individual creators within that common context.

The frequencies and values embodied in those who birth an environment are needed to sustain the life of that environment. Each creator is a donor for the full life of the system. Their beingness will be called upon to support or realign the reality system, if support or realignment is needed. Creating a new context can involve infinite responsibility.

When Beings create a new environment and inhabit it, it is much like the process of building the house of your dreams. You have an idea or a need that inspires you. You feel compelled to realize it. You develop detailed plans for what you envision. As the process progresses, you continue to reconceive your plan to accommodate possibilities and limitations you did not anticipate. It is not until you actually inhabit your house that you experience the gestalt of your dreams, ideas and accommodating choices. Only then do you begin to know what it really means to be the creator of your reality—how well it works, the impact of your choices, and how your nature is reflected in ways you did not anticipate. Living in the house you learn how the environment you have created, in turn creates your experience—adding yet another dimension to your creation of your own experience.

Every conception requires a different prioritization of values for its realization. Imagine that you are inspired with a plan for making profound discoveries about the nature of *gender*. To fulfill this plan you would have to be able to live a lifetime as a man and a lifetime as a woman at the same time, with simultaneous consciousness of both experiences. Earth does not seem to be a suitable context for exploring this particular potential. If there were no existing system of reality in the Universe whose variables were compatible with your objective, you would be prevented from fulfilling this potential for self-realization. Limiting potential is inconsistent with the fundamental creative nature of the Universe. All energy is endowed with the capacity to attract what it requires for transformation and realization. This is the nature of *Sympathetic Vibrational Magnetism.* It is an all-inclusive principle.

Outside your awareness there may be other Beings in the Universe who are inspired to realize potentials that require the same context your gender explorations would require. In order to make innovative discoveries about the nature of *authority,* one Being might need to live simultaneous lifetimes as father and son within the same family constellation. In order to make innovative discoveries about *rhythms of change,* another Being might need to live simultaneous lifetimes in the Dark Ages, the Renaissance and the 21st Century. Each of you has different discovery objectives. However all of you require a reality system that enables you to consciously experience simultaneous multiple manifestations of your identity. This common thread of conception is the stimulus for formulating a new reality context. Your shared intention is the magnetic force that will draw you together with one another. It will also draw to your collective the energy that is necessary to manifest its conception—if the conception becomes integrally aligned among you.

In actuality, such a group of Beings would likely be spread throughout the Universe, with aspects of themselves represented in various forms of embodiment. They would be as capable of collaborating telepathically as by physically gathering in one place. For the purpose of this explanation, however, we are going to imagine these Beings are all people currently living on the Earth with you.

Suppose you have eleven people gathered in your living room. You have discovered that all of you need the same context to pursue your conceptions, but that context does not currently exist. How will you create it? Humanity's standard approach of discussion, design and compromise, provides no one with their vision and everyone with something more limited than their potential. As a group enlightened to the alchemy of creation you might enjoy the discussion, but you would neither impose design nor seek compromise. Instead, you would pursue a process most closely approximated in the councils of Native American ancestors. Sitting together in a circle, you would establish your common intent. Once this was accomplished, you would begin to share your life stories as the moment called them forth from each of you. When the stories quieted among you, you would sit in silent contemplation together, allowing the messages your collective intent had magnetized into story to distill within you and attune you to their values. You would not seek conclusion or look for oracular meaning because you would know, without doubt, the process will provide you with clear, direct knowing at the appropriate moment. Finally, each of you would inhabit the feelings and values of your own vision of living conscious simultaneous lives that inform one another.

On each occasion that your collective gathers in this way of council to inhabit and attune its common intent, your insight would deepen. The intentions and motivations of each of you would become more discerned. Through your own stories and the stories of your collective you would better align your-selves with one another and with the highest values of your intent. In the receptivity of your silent contemplation, your respective individual consciousness and your collective energy field would stimulate each of you into greater awareness. With this increasing and unifying awareness, as each of you inhabits the feelings and values of your own intent, you would be redefining and aligning yourself for the inclusion of all.

If the Souls represented in the collective are integrally aligned toward a common purpose, one of these gatherings will pro-duce unification of their individualized intentions. When this happens, all Beings in the circle will spontaneously conceive their own intent and desire in a way that includes all other Beings in the circle. From this state of being, the pursuit of alignment will give way to merging and unification and the fundamental values of a new context will be constellated.

Such a fundamental alignment and merging of frequencies creates a syntropy that exceeds what was consciously intended by any of its individual contributors. It releases an enormous amount of energy. The collective stimulus that is launched in this state of unified intent magnetizes and organizes the energy that will manifest the new reality context. The final form, while inherent to the integral alignment of the values and frequencies of its creators, is unknowable until it is manifest. Such is the process of collective conception. From it a context of reality is born.

───────────── ∾∾ ─────────────

This example is drawn from a genuine occurrence of collective creation involving Humanity and the Earth. Since the Earth was already able to provide the context for all conditions except conscious awareness of simultaneous manifestations of self, there was no need to create a new reality context. All that was needed was the creation of an adjunct dimension of consciousness in which Beings could consciously experience multiple manifestations of their identity and make meaningful the enlightenment forthcoming from simultaneous lives.

Once it is inhabited by those who have created it, a new dimension becomes available to all who can align with its values and successfully inhabit them. To all others it remains invisible, an unknown dimension of reality—until their own intentions or desires enable them to join the conception, or until they spontaneously align with it through *Sympathetic Vibrational Magnetism.* You might wonder what it would be like if you spontaneously landed in this new dimension of Earth's reality, where it is natural to experience simultaneous manifestations of self. You might experience a past life, another aspect of your Soul identity, or another form of your Being. This is what altered states are made of—inhabiting dimensions of reality with which you are not usually aligned.

Reality systems are not islands. Because all contexts are based upon Universal values, a new context affects the whole of the Universe. Earth was generated from the common vision of all Beings whose frequencies and values formulated her origin and fundamental nature. Her life is integral with all life in the Universe. Her nature is open to be inhabited by all Beings. In conforming their beingness to her nature they bring their own frequencies and values from Earth's potential into Earth's actuality.

The oneness of that which is within you and without you is still only theoretical for most people. You do not yet compre- hend that you actually are the trees and the earth and the ocean and the carbon and the oxygen and the snails and the fish, which you refer to as your environment. You do not yet comprehend that every level of your environment, from the most microcosmic to the most macrocosmic, was created by the frequencies and values of the same Beings who later came to inhabit your environment and be called Human Beings. You have created the Earth. *Full comprehension of this will change the thinking and way of life on your planet. Progres- sing toward this realization is of equal value to arriving.*

Is there life after death?

*W*HEN YOU GO TO SLEEP at night, do you think something is wrong because you are not awake? When you wake up in the morning, do you feel something is wrong because you are no longer sleeping? Of course not. It does not concern you when you are sleeping that you are not awake, or when you are awake that you are not sleeping. When you enter either experience you are fully involved in that experience. When you come home from a full day's work, take off your clothes and step into a soothing shower, you do not feel disoriented. You do not think that something is wrong, that you should still be at work, or that your reality is lost because you left the work world where you were wearing clothes and stepped into the soothing world of running water where you are naked. The fact that it would be outrageously inappropriate for you to appear in either situation in the other condition does not even come to mind. You change from one organization of reality to another all day long without feeling inappropriate or lost. As other dimensions become familiar to you, you will shift among them just as naturally.

There are dimensions that precede, dimensions that follow, dimensions that surround, and dimensions that live within every experience you will ever have. Unless you are conscious of your multidimensionality, when you are focused in any set of dimensional coordinates it is the whole of your frame of reference. It can seem to be the whole of reality.

The Human body is like a body of thought or a body politic; it is everchanging. When you are an adult you do not mourn the loss of your five-year old body, nor do you worry because your teenage body has ceased to be. You accept the transformations from wee baby to toddler, young child to adolescent, and adult to senior, as natural. Yet, where did all those bodies go? Where are those manifestations you were once so invested in? These changes and disappearances are no greater or lesser than changing from a Human body to a light body, or assuming any other state of embodiment. When you pass from any one state of being into any other you become completely involved in the new state. It is a spontaneous response.

Since every dimension of the Universe has the potential to include every other, you can access the whole of the Universe from wherever you are. You need want for nothing. The grass is not greener on the *other side*. There really is no other side. Everything is available to you from wherever you are—if you choose to expand your awareness, experience and understanding to include it.

Those who perceive the presence of Beings who are not in Human form have empirical evidence of life beyond death. For at least as many years as America has been a country, the Spiritualist community in Great Britain has been successfully dedicated to proving the continuance of life. Many mediums in the Spiritualist tradition are able to dramatically demonstrate the continuance of identity beyond death. Contacting those who are no longer alive in their Human bodies, they are able to relay intimate images and information from these Beings—regarding both the past and the present. The mediums who convey this evidence are often disregarded because their personal ideologies burden the proof. This also happens with thousands of healings that never come to the public attention. It is easy for a respected journalist to report on a tumor that disappears after an innovative healing process. It is not as easy if it disappears after an innovative healing process that was accompanied by obscure invocations or chanting, and facilitated by unseen Cosmic helpers.

There are many forms of embodiment in the Universe. There are also many states of being wherein identity is conscious but not expressed through a body. Each state is different from all others in its experience. When you are identified with any state of being you experience yourself as being in that state, whether you are actually alive in that state or not. When people die and find that they have not ceased to be, they continue to experience themselves and to interact with other Beings as if they still had the substantive bodies with which they last identified.

In the states after death, those who have completed a Human embodiment no longer have the sensory system of the Human body. Instead, a projected type of sense memory carries on until they are adjusted to the sensibilities of their new state of being. Before the adjustment fully occurs, most people experience themselves in younger and healthier versions of their Human bodies than the ones they inhabited just before death.

People who strongly identify with the energy, light or Soul state of their Being often make fluid transitions out of their Human state. Those who did not identify well with their Human body often find comfort identifying with their light body or Soul. Interestingly, these people are likely to again direct their consciousness into Human embodiment.

If you think of yourself as someone with curly hair, blue eyes and fat ankles, or someone with unresolved relationships and unfulfilled dreams, you are likely to continue creating life experience within the Human context. When you have come to love yourself without qualification and to experience yourself as a presence, a focalizer of love, or any other metaphor for your essential value, you are more likely to entertain other states of being.

All states of being are equal relative to their purposes.

Changing to a new form of embodiment is, in itself, not necessarily an advancement. It is not greater or lesser to explore consciousness through one system or another. It is, however, reflective of a more advanced consciousness to comprehend the option of assuming other forms of embodiment, and to have the identity security to pursue this option.

An identity that is between embodiments is like a batch of pasta dough. As yet unformed, the dough contains all possible states of being pasta. It has the potential to become rigatoni, spaghetti, linguini, lasagna, fettucini, angel hair, mostacioli, radiatore, or shells. Even though it has this vast potential, until a commitment is made its potential remains conceptual. It has no *formulated* system within which to experience and express its pastahood. Selfhood never ceases; it transforms and transmutes. Even in the state of being pasta dough between embodiments, or between systems of embodiment, there is selfhood. In most cases, however, the experience in between is more like planning or reflecting on a trip than actually taking one.

Once a Being formulates an intent to manifest that is integrally aligned with a system of reality, the Being is prepared to express its frequency/value and Soul resources through a new state of identity. From that point on, the new identity of the Being will be informed of the nature of All That Is as it constellates in the chosen reality system. If Human beingness has been chosen, this *in-formation* process will take approximately nine months. During that time the incarnating Being will be broadcasting its own unique frequency/value into the vibrational field of the Earth, energetically making a path for itself. The incoming identity will be bound by the values of its new reality system until it has fulfilled its local nature and expanded to include other dimensions of reality, or until it has completed its cycle of manifestation in that form and moved on once again through death or transmutation.

Yes, there is life after death—and there is more life after that.

Do people need to surrender free will
to discover their spiritual nature?

*I*N ITS MOST PROFOUND SERVICE free will enables you to live the life of the Creator, to be the source of your own universe of reality. Free will is an artful endowment, a tool for innovation that enables the potentials of nature to be expressed. Through it the subtleties and nuances of All That Is come to be discovered and manifest with everchanging variety. Free will is meant to be an adjunct to the inherent intelligence and instincts of your Being. However Humankind is currently preoccupied with the power and ramifications of free will, and distracted from the inherent values it is meant to express.

As creators who are empowered by free will you have collectively produced a reality you do not respect. Attributing these willful creations to Human nature, rather than to Human unconsciousness, diminishes your respect for yourself, Humanity, free will and nature. This causes you to suffer. People suffer when they freely and willfully make choices that diminish them.

Choices of self-limitation are often made when a person or a collective is overwhelmed, confused or wants to avoid the responsibility of self-expression. They can also be made from a misconception of humility or a misconception of service to others: martyrdom. Regardless of what instigates them, the denial or desensitization necessary to live within self-limiting choices puts you to sleep. You have willed yourself into temporary numbness. In this grogginess your will is deadened to the stimuli of inspiration and inner-direction. This mind/spirit separation allows you to think about your options without being inspired to action.

When the mind/spirit union is *dis-integrated* the exploration of new ground is traded for the maintenance of survival. Like a bear in hibernation, your sleep will last until the threat to your survival has ended and you feel a renewed hunger for life. This usually happens when the sleep of denial, desensitization or delusion becomes more of an entrapment than whatever suffering it is employed to avoid. Fortunately, awakening is a natural impulse and any sleep can unexpectedly become the source of a dream of renewal, insight or liberation.

Even if you have no intention of growing in consciousness and you do nothing purposeful to expand your understanding of All That Is, matriculation from childhood to seniority will produce growth in your consciousness and understanding. When you do not make growth-producing choices at the conscious level of your will, the fundamental magnetism of your superconscious and your subconscious makes them anyway. Your superconscious will draw you toward that which fulfills your purposes for being alive on Earth. Your subconscious will draw you toward self-mastery of that which inhibits you—by frequently producing it, actually or metaphorically.

When you are not taking responsibility for being the creator of your experience, it is likely you will not notice or value what is attracted to you by your subconscious and superconscious magnetism. Having so abandoned yourself, your will drags like a weight that your subconscious and superconscious mind have to pull along in order to do their job. This makes their rates of attraction far slower than when you are actively engaged in choice-making and your will is a propelling force. The slowing of rhythm in the production of personal reality, coupled with the likelihood that superconscious and subconscious creations will go unnoticed, leaves most people who abdicate choice feeling depressed, disengaged and without a niche or a reason to be.

It is important to remember that the choice to cede the privilege of choice, the abdication that results in feeling abandoned, and the stasis that seems meaningless, are not failures. Such interludes are self-created to secure survival. They have value and integrity within your process of self-discovery. In these interludes it does not matter whether the threat to your survival is perceived or actual. With your free will disengaged from inspiration and creative action, even recognition that a threat is illusory does not dissolve it. Discernment of its source will be valuable only after you reawaken and reengage your free will and its empowerments.

Regardless of whether you create or abdicate, nature provides an informative context for your experiences. Her feedback is ever-present. She will talk to you even if you are not talking with yourself. If it is time for you to speak your preferences and you are unwilling, everywhere you go they will serve you cold liver stew!

If life is informative by nature, why not let nature make choices for you? Why not let "the forces that be" move you as they will? If you defer personal choice to the workings of nature, you will be moved along by nature's fundamental forces. If you are not too deeply asleep, you could feel her rhythms, see her patterns and experience her unfettered expression. Such knowledge of external nature can greatly inform you of your internal nature, should you look to it for this purpose. However, while you are moving on nature's elemental course, she could toss you about on wild waters or spin you about in wild winds. To comfort yourself in the magnitude of her expression, you will eventually have to make choices. Whether you grab a limb, seek shelter or learn to read her signs, she will give your power back to you, teaching you that *assertion of free will is an integral part of nature.*

If instead of abdicating and riding nature's tides you think you can remain still, you are mistaken. There is no such place as *still.* All energy is constantly moving. Only the absence of awareness can produce the illusion of stillness. Even for those who are enlightened, the internal stillness produced by their masterful inclusiveness exists concurrently with the constant movement of nature.

If you do not engage your will in your own creative process of choice, you can be easily manipulated by the will and choices of others. In giving up your freedom to make choices that are based on the inner-direction of your own nature, you become one of the defaulting army of people being manipulated by the agenda of a few. The vested interests of fewer than 10,000 people control the worldly variables affecting your planetary population of more than six billion people. Those whose interests rule are not the visible leaders. Their type of power trades in control rather than leadership.

Those who believe their way should be the agenda for everyone can easily collectivize their will and define a course of action. Their sense of themselves as possessing a superior ideology feeds a certainty in them that is illusive to those who do not presume to know but seek to learn. This enables them to demonstrate righteousness sincerely. Theirs is a far more visible position than non-prescriptive tolerance. For those who seek a way that includes the freedoms of all people, it is far more difficult to define a course of unified action. The more diverse your life experiences, the more you value the freedom to originate your own course. The more you see the multidimensionality and validity of all paths, the harder it is to know how to govern freedoms. No judgments are being made about the world's liberal and conservative constituencies in this assessment. Constituencies are founded upon beliefs, not necessarily upon nature.

In some religious and spiritual contexts free will has come to be characterized as a seductive force, responsible for divergence from the path of divinity or enlightenment. It is suggested that surrender of individual free will is the means to unification with higher powers of divinity or enlightenment. You cannot transcend that which you have not mastered.

Your free will enables you to experiment, learning your way to self-mastery. In this process of experimentation you can discover, empirically, the all-inclusive nature of love and its power to enlighten. As your self-expression aligns with your Soul identity the distinction between your personal will and "divine will" disappears. The question of whether to assert or surrender your will, dissolves. The dilemma dissolves not because you have finally come to some "right" way to be, but because you have finally come to the expression of your essential nature.

Before you align the personal and Universal aspects of your nature no one can adequately describe to you this unified self. No one is put together just the way you are. No one has the same purposes for living life as a Human in this era. Many religious and spiritual disciplines chart a path for others to follow. These paths are designed to lead you to love, devotion and right action—as they are experienced, imagined or valued within the discipline. Your challenge is to realize love, devotion and right action as they are uniquely born and revealed in you. This is the way of those whose lives have inspired religious and spiritual disciplines. Until you embrace the inner-direction and courage to do that, you may find guidance and comfort on the paths of others.

Nature sustains and recycles herself ongoingly, inherently preserving her well-being. Human nature, as one of the manifest expressions of nature, has the same capacity. It also has the capacity for free will. When free will becomes controlling rather than cooperative, the willful use of intelligence can override Humanity's inherent capacity to preserve its own well-being.

The use of free will to *control* yourself and others, rather than to *liberate* yourself and others, is a common occurrence in most of your lives. Imagine that it is Thursday night. Your father, who lives out of town, calls to tell you he is coming to visit your sister for the weekend. She lives about an hour's drive from you. Your dad tells you how much he is looking forward to being with his family, that your sister has an extra room ready for you and that she has promised to make the banana cream pie you all used to die for.

When the phone rang you were sitting in your favorite spot staring at nothing, doing nothing, too tired even to think about anything. It took an effort to muster a friendly tone and voice the "Hello" required by the telephone. For several days your glands have been swollen. You have been massaging them, dosing with Vitamin C and planning to take care of yourself over the weekend—plenty of rest, healthy food, relaxation.

Every fiber of your Being knows it is time to stay home, drink tea, rest and be quiet. Instead, you tell your dad you would love to see him, committing to a weekend during which you will expend a lot of energy, talk late into the night and eat banana cream pie. You do not want to hurt your dad's feelings and you do not have the energy or the psychological skills to work out all the old ideas and feelings that have set up these patterns of dishonesty, manipulation and departure from integrity between you.

In order to maintain the feelings everyone believes everyone else should have—even though they are not the feelings anyone does have—you are choosing to ignore your own body and your own feelings. You are choosing to stifle your knowing voice…and later wonder why that voice is so hard to hear. Your sister, operating under similar misguided notions of love, is going to bake banana cream pies even though her family has not eaten sugary desserts for almost a year. Your dad is going to continue to recreate the past as a way of expressing his current love, because no one knows how to change this family dynamic. For fear of hurting someone else no one will risk authentic self-expression. Even though it is the only means anyone has for revelation of the integrity of life, everyone is afraid to trust that the highest good is best served by honest expression. Everyone is afraid to surrender control. This is a transformable Human predicament. Getting yourself into this predicament and getting yourself out of it are in the domain of your free will.

When you are trapped in protecting others' feelings through behavior that causes different suffering than it prevents, the meaning and integrity of life are undermined. For fear of surrendering control, your potential gets lost in the chasm between your Being and your behavior.

The expectations that produce this entrapment are taught and learned. They are not natural. This way of relating is an old idea. It has been tested and it does not work. To cope with the insecurity and distrust of a society that does not sufficiently value you, you are faced with a choice: to surrender all fear and proceed according to inner-direction, or to attempt to control the factors that comprise your vulnerability. The more commonly made choice is control. This choice results in the prescription of behavior for yourself and others. Most importantly, it results in the conscription of youth to well-trodden paths and imposed models of behavior that have already demonstrated themselves to be antithetical to self-realization and Soul alignment. Something truer to nature must be reclaimed and taught.

If you choose to ignore your inner-direction and highest values, no matter how good your reason, you will live in a reality that feeds reason and starves you of value. Even if you suffer under your inner-directed choices, you will empower yourself to make new choices that are informed by the old choices and by your integrity. If you relinquish your power to exercise inner-directed choice, you can do nothing about your suffering until the rest of the world changes.

─────────────────────── ∽∾ ───────────────────────

There is nothing faulty in the nature of free will. Free will endows each of you with the choice to produce suffering or to liberate yourself from it. It is not just what happens, but how you receive and respond to the variables of your life, that determines your experience. When a television antenna is not centered on its axis, reception is significantly altered. If you do not realize your free will has gone askew and your values are misaligned, you will not know that your reception of life is less than it could be. You may assume that what you are receiving is as good as it gets. Many people take that attitude about their unfulfilling lives. Attempting to repair the television set will not resolve the problem of poor reception when a skewed antenna is the cause. Nor will your suffering be resolved by relieving stress through athletics, indulgence or distraction. It ultimately prolongs your suffering to busy yourself treating the symptoms of misalignment rather than treating the cause.

So long has Humankind's assertion of free will been askew, you have amassed a whole raft of imagined needs and inventions to compensate for the shortcomings of your reception of life. By now Humanity can hardly afford to align the antenna. From the point of view of your misaligned values, there is almost too much at stake to stop the suffering. The population of Earth has built a commercial reality and way of life around the assumption that life is faulty, that it requires external mechanisms to sustain it and to make it worth living. Much of the daily life and energy of society are spent producing and utilizing external inventions for a better life. Industry perpetuates itself on the products of your disregard for nature. The better life you imagine—and which you have been groomed to imagine—is dependent upon these products, but the experience of fulfillment and meaningful connectedness requires few of them, so few that everyone could have access to them now.

You are creating your life, consciously or otherwise. It is a misconception that your will gets in your way and that the path of spiritual development is to surrender the will. If you are open to self-discovery, your will is your way. By trusting its course you produce a reality that reveals you to yourself and gives you the feedback necessary to mature yourself into a Universal Being. Bit by bit, fulfilling its purpose, the will transforms into willingness and uses itself up. It has worked its way to essence. It has not surrendered its way.

Do people need to surrender free will to discover their spiritual nature?

*Where do people go
when they are dreaming
or out-of-body?*

*W*HERE HAVE YOU BEEN when you suddenly realize you have not been conscious of driving your car, yet you somehow got where you were going on automatic pilot? Where are you when the experience you are having while sleeping or meditating feels too real to be a dream?

Experiences of nonordinary reality and encounters with Beings from the Greater Universe require a shift of your focus, intensified magnetism, or increased frequency amplitude. When something that was invisible to you suddenly becomes self-evident, you have expanded in at least one of these ways. All passages into nonordinary states involve the transit of your consciousness, and sometimes your body, through what is known as *astral space*.

Astral space is a transitional zone within and surrounding each planetary and dimensional reality system in the Universe. It is not an astral "plane" as it is often called, but an integral network of dimensional spaces, or zones. Astral zones provide a similar function for all Beings in the Universe, not just Human Beings. They are transitory zones of consciousness where temporal realities are created by those who have cause to produce them.

In some instances astral space serves only as a passageway to other dimensions of Universe reality—a stop on the subway line that the express train passes through without pause. In other instances astral space is the traveler's destination. And sometimes a traveler who intended to pass through on the express, becomes engaged in the goings-on of astral space and transfers to the local.

Difficult and dualistic experiences of nonordinary reality, such as the recreation of disturbing or incomplete past events in order to resolve them, occur within *astral space. Nonordinary experiences that fill you with feelings of renewal or illumine you to the oneness of the Universe and your own creatorship within it, occur* beyond *astral space. They are accessed through your superconscious or Soul.*

Astral space can be loosely compared with the subconscious dimension Humans have created. You have developed your sub-conscious as a limited context for experiences that you are not pre-pared to integrate. It allows you to exclude aspects of your reality from your immediate conscious experience and responsibility. The subconscious has specific confines. A person's subconscious reality is not ordinarily apparent to others. It does not ordinarily occupy physical space and time. It is an alternate focus for consciousness rather than a primary one. And while its content may be meaningful to others, it is singularly experienced.

Astral zones *differ* from your subconscious in that several Beings can interact in a shared temporal experience that wholly resembles reality. Experiences produced in astral zones have no apparent impact on Beings who are not there. They can, however, have a profound unseen impact. If Hitler were to reconcile his past in an Astral dramatization, the historic force of religious persecution would diminish in the world and a Human collective would experience healing.

Each ongoing reality system in the Universe is founded upon a uniquely integrated and different organization of the same values. Astral space is the only exception. It is the only inter-active space in the Universe with no predefined organization of Universal values. This unique condition allows it to equally serve Beings from different reality systems with different organizations of values. Its nature is to reflect whatever you bring to it.

This reflective nature is why some people experience danger, hostility and conflict in astral space. Unaccustomed to moving out-of-body or outside ordinary states of consciousness, the experience may awaken their fears. This causes them to look for threats, dangers or adversaries. Looking for them both formulates an astral context for their appearance and projects them. Returning to ordinary states of consciousness after such an experience, people often conclude that there are ghouls and evil forces rampant in astral space. It is, of course, just as easy to formulate a context for interaction with angels, mythological characters or past loved ones who may be available to astral space. Whatever is experienced in astral space is a reflection of the intrapsychic state of the astral traveler. This does not mean it is imagined; it is fully real while it is happening.

Experiences created as a reflection of the intrapsychic mind are characterized in numerous classic tales. Heroes and heroines enter extraordinary realities to produce and overcome their fears and limitations. Will Odysseus surmount the Sirens, Siddhartha liberate himself from the compelling attractions of sensual pleasure, and Luke Skywalker overcome his self-doubt, to realize the values to which they aspire?

Having no predefined organization of values, astral space permits simultaneous temporary constructions of realities that would not normally exist in the same dimensions. You could be the adult you currently are, watching yourself as a child interacting with your grandfather, who died before you were born. This is much like the transition space between waking and dreaming, where you are able to weave aspects of one reality with the other, or like a border town where two distinct cultures overlap.

Until someone arrives projecting a reality, there is nothing in astral space but potential. As soon as someone projects a theme or value into astral space, other Beings in the Universe who can make use of its context have an opportunity made available to them. Often they are drawn to it unconsciously, the way you get to a dream.

Astral space can fulfill needs that your waking life cannot satisfy. If you are ready to go forward into greater depths of community, but you have not completed your attraction to the territorialism characterized in the American Wild West, you can satisfy your territorialism by acting it out in astral space. If momentary daily oppressions raise in you the fierce inequities of slavery, you can claim your equality by recreating Civil War abolitionism in astral space. By acting out roles in this transitional space, Beings do not have to invest a lifetime in setting up circumstances for resolutions that are tangential to their life purposes, but inhibiting their fulfillment. They can have real experience in condensed time, in a simulated environment—so long as the projection progresses on course.

An astral projection is an inherently unstable environment. It is always a bit of a crap shoot as to how long your consciousness will maintain the focus necessary for it to remain coherent. There is also the question of how well it will continue to conform to your native reality system if others enter it with their own projections. How long it stays coherent determines whether you will be able to complete your projected experience or get booted out of the theater before resolution in the third act. How well it conforms to your home reality system determines how meaningful the experience will be and how successfully it will integrate into your consciousness.

No matter where you are in the Universe or where you are in the development of your consciousness, transformative experience requires physical, emotional, psychological, intellectual, transpersonal and spiritual integration. If you stir up a drama in astral space and return to ordinary reality before the drama is complete, you may evoke something from your subconscious mind that has no conscious context for resolution. An interrupted projection like this can be difficult to integrate. Even though some projections are not coherently completed, many are profoundly successful. Beings throughout the Universe continue to play the odds.

Just as *virtual reality* allows you to drive the Indianapolis 500 or walk through a real estate property in another city without leaving your living room, astral space allows you to move beyond memories and imaginings into direct experience of their reality. Astral experiences do not feel like theatrical constructions while they are happening. Once you identify with an astral projection the experience feels as real as your life. That is what makes it possible to have meaningful and integral experiences in astral space. Even if you are aware that you are in an altered state, the stimuli are so real that you will likely stop observing and become fully engaged by the compelling relevancy of the experience.

Because astral space is inherently more volatile than a constant and coherent reality system, it is conducive to manifestation of the disruptive and competitive states found in dualistic realities. It is almost impossible to maintain an inverted or misaligned value within a fully coherent individual consciousness or collective reality system. If Beings within an advanced reality system become engaged in misalignment, the energy of the misalignment will temporarily separate them from their integral environment. Experiencing a brief loss of coherence, they spontaneously relocate to an astral zone where it is possible to contextualize and work out the mis-aligned value. This relocation is as natural as an ice cube turning to water in the sun because the sun's warmth does not sustain ice. It is neither bad nor good, just as the ice cube is not bad or good for melting. There are no judgments connected with transitional spaces. This spontaneous relocation to astral space is not frightening or disorienting to advanced beings. It is a familiar process that is embraced as self-revelatory and self-healing.

———— ∽∾ ————

It is unusual for a person to have difficulty returning to their ordinary consciousness from an astral projection—as unusual as waking up while you are still in your dream and not being able to exit it immediately. To get stuck in an astral projection your ordinary state of consciousness would have to be in such extreme disorganization that you could not identify with it well enough to reintegrate it. This can happen when your ordinary state has been altered disruptively by drugs or by a fundamental violation, such as severe abuse, deprivation or fear. If historic fundamental violations are reactivated in a projection that loses coherence before it is completed, this too could cause an extreme discontinuity, making it difficult for you to reidentify with your ordinary consciousness. What your society calls Multiple Personality Disorder is a product of such disruption and interruption, producing simultaneous, inconstant manifestations of personal reality.

———— ∽∾ ————

For Humans to experience the Greater Universe or for Beings from the Greater Universe to experience your reality, each must travel through transitional zones of astral space without becoming caught in a projection. If you do not get caught up, astral space can be an open highway to locations beyond: other planets and other dimensions of yourself and the Greater Universe.

In its own way, astral space provides a self-discovery and preparatory zone that insures a traveler's readiness to experience other dimensional and planetary realities. If your projections preoccupy you, you are not ready to go beyond them and astral space will give you an opportunity to clean house. If you are internally secure in your identity and coherent enough in your consciousness to experience another reality system, you can move through astral space without notice of it. You have no emotional, psychological or mental hooks to get caught on in passage. When passage is unobstructed, astral space serves to transform your frequency and/or magnetism for function within another system of reality —like an adapter that allows you to use a 110 volt/50 cycle appliance, in a 220 volt/60 cycle electrical outlet.

In astral space it is possible to experience conditions that are not commonly expressed in your local reality system, but are natural to other life forms and other dimensions of the Universe. When the astral transformer has done its job successfully, you are not disoriented by altered conditions like timelessness, condensed and expanded time, role reversals, telepathy and interspecies communication.

> *The omnipresence of Universal values enables you to experi-*
> *ence yourself as a constant, no matter where you go in the*
> *Universe. Even when the external manifestation of a value is*
> *changed into something unfamiliar, the stimuli it communi-*
> *cates and the feeling and intellectual responses you have to*
> *it will remain constant. You take your "home system" of*
> *consciousness with you wherever you go in the Universe,*
> *unless you willingly surrender it to identify with a different*
> *system of reality.*

Universe Beings who have transcended dualistic reality rarely participate in transitional astral dimensions. When we do engage, it is to facilitate self-healing or the healing and experimentation of others. We use astral space primarily as a cosmic highway to get us from one system to another.

As you become more familiar with the nature of astral space and its process of transit, you will gain the discernment to use it purposefully. It can become a conscious tool to accelerate your personal healing or experimentation. And, as a frequent flyer, you will learn to more readily access other reality systems within the Greater Universe.

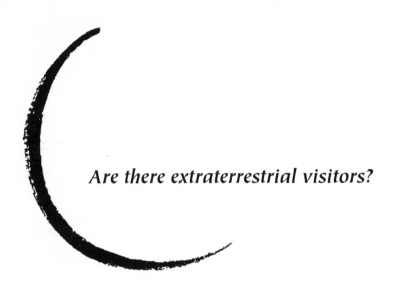

Are there extraterrestrial visitors?

*B*EINGS FROM THE Greater Universe have always been in contact with Earth and her people. We have been capable of reaching you from the dawn of your civilization. We have, in fact, joined you periodically in those times and places throughout history where popular thinking allowed for our existence. Evidence of these visits is found in your many artifacts showing winged Beings or Beings who travel in winged vehicles.

More recently in your time continuum Beings from the Greater Universe, most of whom were not enlightened Universal Beings, have interacted with members of Earth's governmental and scientific communities. Because of the exclusivity of these meetings and the belief systems of those involved, what resulted was primarily intrigue and confusion, accompanied by a minimal exchange of information and technology. You would not be as advanced in general technology or space travel as you are today without the materials and information derived from extraterrestrial visitors. Industrial materials that are in popular use and propulsion technology for your space program have been reverse-engineered from the hardware of these sources.

The people who participated in these meetings with Beings from the Greater Universe, or who were involved in the events surrounding these meetings, are scattered. Some of them are unwilling to identify themselves. Several have already died. Incomplete information regarding these historic meetings between worlds has been uncovered by your contemporary UFO investigators. Unfortunately, many within this devoted and informal research community have identified themselves as the "good guys" fighting against the "bad guys"—repressive government—to uncover the truth and reveal it to Humanity. Their participation in this adversarial model feeds the collective distrust that surrounds the subjects of ETI (Extraterrestrial Intelligence) and UFOs (Unidentified Flying Objects). At least as importantly, this dualism sorely inhibits their potential for Universal assistance in their mission—which is also a Universe mission. Rather than overcome or outwit those who are opposed to their efforts, we wish these truth seekers would overcome the adversarial positions within themselves. This would better align them with advanced Universe Beings and enable magnetism *(SVM)* to facilitate their direct conscious experience of EETI (Enlightened Extraterrestrial Intelligence).

Recent American governments have been less than repressive of historic information regarding these historic extraordinary events. They have been unaware or uninformed. Let us assure you that the interdimensional opportunities close at hand for Humanity are far superior to those caught in the mire of this historic intrigue. Given one broadly experienced interaction with advanced Universe Beings, the mystery and confusion of those past moments will dissolve.

There is good reason why the people of Earth are not further progressed in reaching other life in the Cosmos. The models and ideas currently dominating your society are capitalistic and competitive rather than humanistic and cooperative. The technology you are able to develop from these inverted values will not enable you to access the more enlightened populations of the Universe. The vibrational construction of your ideas and your hardware is not sympathetic with the physical and mental environments you seek to reach. It is too dense.

When advanced extraterrestrial civilizations pursue the development of technology, they study the nature of Universal reality to find models for their technological expansion. If an idea cannot be realized in concert with the environment, they toss it out as an unsatisfactory or immature idea. When an idea is found to be consistent with Universal values and local nature, research and development is begun. This self-respecting value system is not legislated. It is the inspiring ethical code of the civilizations that prosper within it. With these controls of integrity, every step of scientific progress produces by-products that expand the well-being and creative options of their societies and the Greater Universe.

It appears that those who pursue technological development on Earth are willing to risk the whole earthly environment to realize the specific goals upon which they are focused at any given time. Instead of honoring nature in an integral way, Humankind currently honors its capacity to manipulate nature to preconceived ends. This eventually produces a reality system based upon manipulation, which severely weakens the intrinsic momentum of the system.

———

Anything created by manipulation has to be maintained by manipulation. Maintaining a manipulated reality system demands constant work to sustain that which has the inherent capacity to sustain itself—in its integrous state.

———

A reality system with Universal integrity fuels itself—as Nikola Tesla knew. Of the other Universe civilizations with material natures comparable to yours, most freely derive their fuels from unlimited passive sources such as crystal magnification and the collection of solar-like energy. By the choices you make, you continue to manipulate nature in order to maintain and sell your supply of fuels. This desire to control nature rather than cooperate with her narrows your perception of alternatives, depriving you of free energy and forcing you to consume natural resources. The planetary cost of this consumption is not recoverable.

———

The natural resources of the Earth are not products for your consumption; they are agents of your preservation. These natural resources are the storehouse of elemental stimuli the Earth uses to regenerate herself. The substances you think of as sellable resources are the physical mediums for alchemical transmutation of environmental poisons, and the conduit for communication of vibrational stimuli and frequencies that secure your planetary stability.

──────────────────── ⌒⌒ ────────────────────

Draining the Earth's elemental tributaries is like draining the blood from your veins. Both organisms, the body and the Earth, are designed to replenish their raw materials in moderation in order to sustain themselves. You can give a pint, but you cannot give a gallon. If you give a gallon, veins collapse. If you drain the Earth, your ground of being destabilizes and the Earth quakes. The tolerances for depletion and the rhythms of replenishment for any natural resource are knowable. They are discrete reflections in the frequency and amplitude of each elemental resource being depleted.

Right now your heart beats, your blood circulates and your body digests and eliminates—with integral momentum. If you want to take over and invent a "better" way for the heart to beat, you will have to invent new working processes for circulation, digestion and elimination. Unless you create an integral self-sustaining system, any singular manipulation of nature takes you away from well-being and the intrinsic momentum required for perpetuation of the whole. This is a fundamental difference between advanced Universe Beings and Human Beings in the comprehension of values, and therefore, in our approaches to technological and other development. It is why you have not reached enlightened communities of extraterrestrial life through your space travel and technology.

Advanced Universe Beings who wish to realize physical community with you await the readiness of your attitudes and receptivity. Because Earth is still a war entangled planet dominated by adversarial and competitive thinking, Universe visitors must be very careful about their timing and mode of entry. The decision of when and where to arrive on Earth is laden with ethical, social and political complexities. We do not want to be claimed or shot by any government, have zoos made for us, or have our images sold as chocolate covered marshmallows.

We are most concerned with producing a means of entry that is nonviolent. This is no small undertaking. Our encounters to date have taught us that violation is in the eye and the belief system of the beholder. If spaceships enter Earth's atmosphere before appropriate trust is established, those of you who think in adversarial and catastrophic terms are likely to produce fear, anxiety and chaos, constructing us as "the enemy."

If we from other dimensions come to Earth looking as we do in our native states, many of us would be invisible to you. Among those who would be visible, some have an appearance quite different from your own. For us to appear without a linear means, or transport vehicle, bearing little or no physical resemblance to you, would strain your logic and tolerances. While these demonstrations are natural to us, they could be an assault to your senses and well-being. They might even be so shocking as to cause a reaction of physical pain or trauma, such as a heart attack. That would be a violent thing to do to another Being. It would be contrary to our regard for all Beings and our wish for benevolent encounters. You might think we could protect you from violent physical reaction to our appearance, but rarely would our values permit us to do that.

We have too much respect for the integrity of your reality system to manipulate it, or to interfere with your organic response patterns.

Because you do not yet realize your own profundity, when we appear before you, you will likely think us more powerful than yourselves. We are Beings who are advanced in manifesting a *different* organization of Universal values than those familiar to most of you. Our advancement is born of our love and our understanding, not of power. Holding us as superior could cause you to feel inferior, inadequate, defensive or endangered. Any of these responses would have a violently disempowering impact on your civilization. We are not violent. Our aspiration is to empower you and free you to join us in further realizing the potential of our shared Universe.

We seek to enter your reality system with respect for your perceptions of time, space, logic, reason, beauty and natural order. For this reason many of us who serve as ambassadors from the Greater Universe have chosen to be born here. It is the only means we have found to fully honor your reality system and dissolve the concerns of potential violence. When a Cosmic Being comes to Earth to live as a Human Being, it is an act of love. If we do not love and respect you enough to *be* you, how could we presume to know you and serve you? Most of us demonstrate no powers or miracles except those naturally born from clarity, understanding, wisdom and love. In living as Humans on the Earth, it is our hope to inform you of your multidimensional nature and the nature of the Universe by inspiring your understanding, catalyzing your memory of Soul knowledge, and *showing you enlightenment in your own image.*

As you progress toward Universal consciousness, communication is growing between Earth and other dimensions of the Cosmos. The people of planet Earth are opening their doors of awareness and expectation. You are beginning to entertain in yourselves the idea of a greater reality. Your collective imagination and your collective dreams are expanding to include us. In your movies and other forms of entertainment you are creating characters of great wisdom who come from dimensions beyond your own. For years you have been asking questions left and right—now you are finally looking up! The search for extraterrestrial intelligence has become science rather than science fiction. We feel you liberating us from your imaginations and beginning to think of us as the real Beings that we are. It is a relief to us.

As your relationship with Cosmic Beings emerges from fantasy and hope into belief, you are bringing thoughts of us into your lives. This brings your lives more into our thoughts. It is the beginning of an intimate relationship.

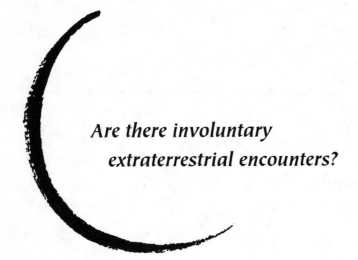

Are there involuntary
extraterrestrial encounters?

*I*T IS NOT A SIMPLE JOB to address your confusion and misconceptions about UFOs, ETI and extraterrestrial encounters. To briefly describe to you the dynamics of Universe populations is like asking you to briefly explain the sociology and cultural anthropology of life on Earth. Nonetheless, offering you a Cosmic view of extraterrestrial encounters and of those who precipitate them, may bring you insight as well as new ways to frame your questions and concerns regarding extraterrestrial encounters.

The notion that an encounter on any level can be involuntary is only partially true. Each of us, regardless of our placement in the Universe, creates the whole of our own experience from the resources of our Being—self, Soul, frequency, value. However, when we abdicate the privilege to create, whether intentionally, through ignorance, or by taking a break from responsibility for ourselves, we allow the creations of others to include us.

If you are sleeping and a cat is about to pounce onto your chest, you could have a wide variety of responses. You may sense it, awaken and move to avoid the interaction. You may sense it, but not trust your subtle senses enough to act, or you may be too deeply asleep or too tired to act. Once you have been pounced upon, you may be so startled by the event that you feel violated. You may be angry, or you may embrace it with humor as a part of the cosmic dance that indeed belongs to you.

You have as wide a range of responses and as great a privilege of choosing attitude and meaning when you are unexpectedly visited by a Being from the Greater Universe. Is it a rare opportunity? A threat to your life? An event in which you are powerless? An event to which you are equal? Do you approach it as an anthropologist, a spiritual seeker, a journalist, a victim, an ethnocentrist, a historian, a pathfinder or a proof seeker?

The increasing interaction between Humans and Beings from the Greater Universe creates a long awaited opportunity. It also makes things more complex for all of us, temporarily. It is a mistake to think that all those from the Greater Universe who are able to visit you are necessarily more enlightened than you are or that a spaceship is any more spiritually sophisticated than a Chevy.

The advanced and the enlightened societies in the Universe are ethically self-governed by their understanding of integrity and the multidimensional creative process. Their wisdom precludes them from interfering with the actions of those who are differently developed than they are. While this means they

do not impose themselves on Humans, it also means they
do not impose themselves on other Beings who do *impose*
themselves on Humans.

———————————————— ∽∾ ————————————————

Those who perpetrate involuntary encounters with Humans are actually few in number. Due to genetic manipulation designed by their ancestors to control behaviors they perceived to be threatening to their society, these Beings are less individuated in mind and emotion than most of us in the Universe. The subjective and emotional resources of their population have been controlled to the point of extinction. Because of this they are unable to perceive their actions as violating your individual sanctity and freedom. As a result of the engineered limitations of their gene pool, the offspring of this manipulation have arrived at a point of risk to their survival. Since Human Beings are the Beings who most closely resemble them as they were before genetic manipulation, they feel collectively compelled to study you. They do not realize that the very attributes they are seeking to recover are the ones they are violating when they impose themselves on you.

It is important to understand that these Beings are not evil. The problem is that they are neither emotional nor relational. They have no need to relate to one another with subjective consideration because they are not emotionally differentiated from one and other. It is their belief that all Beings in the Universe are interdependent. From this they conclude that all Human Beings have implicitly agreed to cooperate with them. Any interaction with a Human that serves the growth of their understanding appears to them to serve the whole Universe. Although these beliefs are currently misconceived in both meaning and application, they reflect essential truths of our multidimensional Universal integralism.

Unable to experience Human modes of intelligence, these uninvited visitors attribute your resistance and fear to lesser intelligence. If you were more intelligent, they believe, you would be as curious about them as they are about you, and eager to interact. Being of one mind, they cannot understand why you do not recognize and comply with their designs for the exchange of information. They do not know what to do when you fail to respond to their telepathy. What for them is a natural and spontaneous compliance, is for you an involuntary submission. Most importantly, they do not understand that the subordinative humility taught by many of your religious, institutional and family systems, as well as the feelings of inadequacy fostered by competition and societal inequities, encourage most Humans to feel inferior when encountering Beings who seemingly have superiority or authority.

In underestimating your intelligence they demonstrate their belief that your differentness makes you inferior. This notion of inequality among Beings is supported by the way you on Earth treat each other. Your manipulation of the less intelligent and less privileged in your society, as well as of other species, sets up the *sympathetic* resonance that enables these Universe Beings to aggress in your reality system as they do. Your behavior aligns with theirs. Given the laws of *Sympathetic Vibrational Magnetism,* it is understandable that your societies are engaging one another in misconceptions of power and domination.

Consider the behavior of those on Earth who engage in the testing and dissection of animals. It is common in your society to regard other species as sources of information whose rights are expendable in service to the greater good. Unfortunately, until you come to higher levels of understanding in regard to your bodies, health and healing, you may not see other choices for research. In the coming years, as you better understand energetic and vibrational health and healing, your current systems of thought and practice will appear primitive to you. Research on other species will become irrelevant and spiritually unacceptable to you.

Those in the Cosmos who wish to assert their agenda over yours are no more adversarial than your fellow Humans who want to do the same thing. They seem more threatening because you cannot size them up. You do not know their game the way you know the manipulations of power and control in your own reality system. Their appearance, physically and conceptually, threatens your notion of reality, and their technology and psychic abilities can be intimidating. Many of you experience yourselves as defenseless against these unknowns and feel fundamentally at risk when you encounter them. Since most people have been raised in competitive models, it is difficult to understand that for the Universe to be greater than you believed, you do not have to be less than you believed.

What can we who are more enlightened do when others' interpretations of truth violate the free will and subjective emotional integrity of Humans and other Beings? Their behavior concerns us greatly, but thus far we have been unable to precipitate their enlightenment to the nature of emotional individuation or to convince them to behave otherwise. They have no resources for comprehending the sanctity of your individuated free will and the vulnerability of your emotional identity. It is difficult for Beings to appropriately value what they have not experienced. We hope you will keep this in mind when it is your turn to meet the unfamiliar.

Since we seek to enlighten rather than control these less developed Beings—just as we seek to enlighten rather than control Human Beings—our choice has been to assist them in their encounters. We refuse to participate *directly* in the invasive experiments of those who undertake such missions. Our role is to minimize the interference, discomfort or violation you experience during these encounters. We are there to serve as facilitators, to relay your thoughts in ways that might be understood by them and to respond to your feelings as best we can, given the circumstances. Our intent in assisting them is to advance their understanding and respect for you as quickly as possible, bringing this epoch of involuntary research to an end. Unwilling to polarize with them, we express our integrity by protecting yours. It is rare that "involuntary" encounters are carried on without one of us present, but it does happen.

There are varying opinions within the Universe as to whether or not we should be assisting in something we do not sanction. For those of us who have lived as Humans or assisted Humans, there is no question. We know that theoretical and principled debate are inappropriate responses to real and immediate fear, pain, hunger, threat or confusion. While we would prefer not to assist those who engage you involuntarily, that would leave you without external support. It would also leave your perpetrators without feedback for self-correction and Universal alignment.

Try thinking of this small aggressive population as adolescents with cars, bank accounts, advanced technologies, collective purpose and as much energy focused in the repression of emotion as your teenagers have in their expression of it. Adolescence is a critical stage of development for maintaining communication. If we polarize with these Beings during this stage, the energy for rebellion and rejection inherent in their adolescent process would jeopardize future dialogue. If we succeed in preserving tolerance of one another and pathways for communication, we secure potentials for long-term relationship.

You may shake your head at the powerful ignorance of these Beings, but you should know that Universal Beings are equally stymied in trying to precipitate Human enlightenment to the nature of *freedom*. You kill one another for it. Because many of you do not yet realize that you are all one, you do not comprehend that eliminating parts of yourself, rather than growing to integrate or enlighten them, *limits* your potential for freedom.

The unenlightened Beings who would try to control you are a small population of the Greater Universe. For the rest of us to try to stop them would be as inappropriate as our trying to stop you from creating crack babies, abusing one another and polluting our shared Universal space. Instead, we hope to inspire you toward higher options by joining with you and assisting you in enlightenment. We are all unenlightened to some extent. Freedom to experiment and to learn from direct experience are ways in which we all progress toward enlightenment. We trust the Universe to sustain the stresses of its self-realization process.

The greater percentage of interactions between Humans and Beings from the Greater Universe are those that are affirming, healing and expanding. Unfortunately, these experiences are less publicized. Because they transpire in love, they integrate so naturally within your hearts and minds that most people do not realize they have actually participated in multidimensional reality and interacted with Universal Beings. People are more likely to identify these experiences as dreams, meditations, visions, mystical experiences or imaginings. When you identify and speak out about your multi-dimensional experiences, you empower yourself by unifying your Being with your behavior. You also help to inform Humanity of the supportive intelligent life that surrounds them in the Universe.

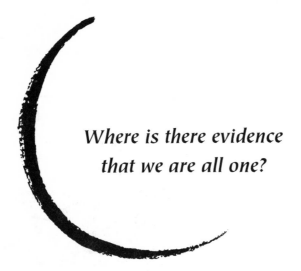

Where is there evidence
that we are all one?

*I*F YOU ARE SEEKING proof that will permit you to believe we are all one, you will regrettably find yourself subject to the tautology "Show me the mountain and I will believe," which calls forth the response: "Believe and you will see the mountain." All knowledge becomes self-evident as the self aligns with All That Is. Only direct experience will take you beyond faith or an intellectual embrace of oneness. The fact that billions of people are simultaneously experiencing unique realities and the world has not collapsed from discontinuity, should be evidence of cooperation within a unified system of vast tolerance and variability. The fact that you can find my experience within you, and I can find yours within me, is another demonstration of the oneness of all things that appear to be separate.

For the moment, imagine All That Is, or God, as a radio. The radio comes assembled to transmit and receive. It is in integrated working order. Suppose the radio wanted to know the nature and potential of each of its parts, without giving any part priority and without ignoring any one part to focus on any other. To do this the radio would have to liberate its parts from fixed placement and given relationships within the whole. It would also have to endow each part with the capacity for autonomous expression, so that all parts could simultaneously explore themselves, their relationships to each other and their collective radiohood. Soon there would be wires, transistors, knobs and dials everywhere, each exploring its nature, intrinsically motivated to fulfill its potential and discover a greater wholeness to which it belongs.

Each Being in the Universe is a unique aspect of the Source that has been endowed with autonomous identity in order that it may simultaneously and freely express its potential in relation to all else that is.

Human Beings find themselves endowed with the capacities and dilemmas of free will and autonomy, as well as with the motivation to fulfill their individual and collective potential. In the Universal dimensions of your origin you are all one, parts of an integral whole. In the current consciousness and dimensional coordinates of Earth you perceive yourselves as separated from one another and even from other manifestations of your own frequency/value in the plant, animal and mineral kingdoms. In fact, your full nature can only be discovered when you include all parts of yourself—and yourself as a part of the whole. No part of the radio can do what a radio does without the other parts. No part of the radio is dispensable. The radio cannot be a radio without each and every one of its parts. Until you come to realize the connectedness of the whole, you will endeavor to find fulfillment as a wire, a knob, a dial or a transistor. This can cause you to feel unfulfilled or disconnected from each other and from your Source.

While the Human radio is getting itself together, you as an individual are not limited by the pace of others' self discovery. Everyone need not reach enlightenment at the same moment in order for *you* to be realized, but everyone must eventually reach enlightenment for *Humanity* to be realized.

The metaphor of the radio is not meant to imply a mechanistic nature to the source known as God, or All That Is. Through the process of disassembling and reassembling the parts of the whole, God is experiencing the many facets of God-nature, simultaneously and in their infinite relationships to one another. This process both reveals and gives expression to the nature of All That Is. It also generates new stimuli for creation as frequencies in the Universe, and as children in the world. The process of God's self-realization is reflected in the experience of each individuated part—each Being in the Universe—as we discover our nature, explore our value and realize that we are God expressed.

Every Being in the Universe, Human or otherwise, is a unique constellation of All That Is. Each of us is a composite containing every value in the Universe. In this way, each person contains all people and each Being embodies the Universe. The values comprising the wholeness of any one of us are expressed in numerous dimensions of reality. It is in embracing our multidimensionality that we can experience the wholeness of our selfhood and the intricate oneness of All That Is. While we are all comprised of the same frequencies and values, no two Beings constellate all the values in exactly the same way. Each of us will put the pieces of the whole together in a different order, generating from our differing streams of consciousness. This resource of combinant values is to the Universe as the gene pool is to Humankind. The number of combinations of essential values may be infinite. Where there are waves of duplication within Beings there is great affinity and camaraderie among those Beings. This is true for all Beings, in all times and all places throughout the Universe.

While all of our lives are derived from one Source that inherently motivates us toward realization of our oneness, you may or may not be living a life whose purpose and design seem like a journey toward enlightenment. Regardless of linear and temporal appearances, every lifetime is created for the purpose of enlightenment. It is rare, however, that any one lifetime manifests the full realization of your Being. More often, self-realization is expressed in the amalgam of all manifestations and life experiences derived from your Soul. You experience this amalgam, your Soul, every time you find yourself knowing something you have no current life experience of learning.

Once you are Universally aligned and have the eyes to see it, oneness is apparent to you at every level of being, from every angle of vision, in every system of reality.

What can be done
to change the world?

*T*HE ALCHEMICAL WAY to change the world is to align yourself with Universal values. To get to alignment from wherever
you are you can employ any all-inclusive and love-centered
discipline or you can commit yourself to meeting each moment with
love, authenticity and openness to self-discovery.

Anything Humanity energizes gains reality in the world.
Anything of Universal value that Humanity energizes can
engage Universal resources.

When you create something that expresses misaligned or inverted
values, its stimuli are entirely contained within the world. This
makes it difficult for the Greater Universe to assist you with healing
responses. When you come to realize that a misaligned construction of collective reality has occurred, it is time to create a medium
or a tool to correct the problem. If you create one that derives from
Universal values, you can tap Universal resources and engage us in
your healing process. So supported, even a small number of you
can initiate powerful corrective stimuli.

Your founding psychologists offer an excellent example of inventing a medium for correcting Humanity's inversion and misalignment of Universal values. Their medium is an all-inclusive conceptual system in which tools can continually be created to address the entrained and acquired misalignments within your consciousness. By including the spiritual and transpersonal dimensions of Human identity, the context of psychology has become a Universal medium, enabling Universal Beings to engage in your processes and support your healing. Even though some values are not yet appropriately prioritized within psychology, its best tools can align you with Universal values and connect you with Soul resources.

While there was an unnamed psychological dimension in the early practice of magic, as well as in Platonic and Aristotelian thought, psychological reality did not integrate into popular Human awareness. It was not until the work of Sigmund Freud that psychological reality became acknowledged. In response to deep internal inquiry Freud had an insight—*a direct knowing*—of values not yet integrated within Human consciousness. Responding to this insight, he offered Humanity a stimulus to expand its awareness to include psychology. Until people began to experiment with this new lens and to experience its value, psychology had no reality in the modern world. When Carl Jung entered the dialogue he brought the Human collective into the psychological model, thereby integrating psychology into collective Human consciousness. Supported by the work of ancestors from pre-history and the ancient world, Freud, Jung and the innovators who followed, formed a collective that succeeded in engaging enough Human consciousness to establish the reality of psychology. It was not until transpersonal values were included that psychology became a Universally supported healing medium.

As you progress into higher frequency amplitudes and toward the transmutation of Human consciousness, many of the psychological tools and processes that have been valuable in your *transition* and *transformation* will become obsolete. The tools of one level can be the limitations of the next. It will not take you generations to invent and establish the personal and social healing systems for which collectives are now forming. The consciousness of the modern world is far more advanced than when Freud began his work. The resources for public communication are available. Your need is conscious and great. And the time has come.

————— ∽∾ —————

You are currently being called upon to create healing processes for all of your social systems. Because few vested economic interests would be jeopardized, public education is an accessible system for transformation. You are challenged to reinvent education as a tool for correcting Human misalignment and for empowering Human potential. To do this you will need to conceive of education as a medium for alignment with Universal values. This will advance rather than supplant internalization of the informational education your civilization has thought of as learning and has promoted.

Do not worry that in opening the pursuit of Universal values you will bump into the conflicting moral values that are established among you. Universal values do not conflict. They are more fundamental than dualistic morality. If values are colliding, rather than seeking union, they are not Universal values and you need to simplify further.

————— ∽∾ —————

As the advent of psychology demonstrates the invention of integral reality, the saga of the American buffalo, or bison, demonstrates how reality that is not energized by Human response ability can become unreal. Prior to 1845 there were 60 million American buffalo. In 1895 there were only 800 left in the world. The buffalo was abandoned to become a remembrance and a mythic figure. If there had not been people who responded to this passing and were willing to devote energy to reestablishing integral relationship with these animal Beings, the American buffalo would be unreal today. Since few people have ever seen or even thought about an American buffalo, you might wonder what difference it would make if these animals disappeared from the world.

Each and every embodiment of life brings to Earth a value of All That Is. Were it not for their Earthly manifestations these values would only be accessible to you through intellectual, meditative or revelatory experience. The discontinuance of any species is the loss of a value from your world. It produces discontinuity in your multidimensionality, weakening the integrity of your planetary reality. Only misaligned and inverted values, such as violence, disrespect, manipulation and dishonesty, are appropriate for extinction. Preserving and honoring each and every Universal frequency and value is essential to your Human and planetary well-being.

Abandonment of a Universal value is within the tolerances of developmental experimentation, but it significantly weakens the integrity of your manifest reality. While the same frequency/value may be manifest in other species within other kingdoms on the Earth, a lost strain of buffalo would mean a lost vibration in Earth's symphonic OM—the field of vibrational resonances that keeps the Earth humming. It would be like Big Ben striking twelve o'clock with eleven real chimes and one imagined. Like a phantom limb, the value manifest as the American buffalo could only be readily felt by those who had once been consciously connected to it.

The loss of essential values and the pain produced by inverted and misaligned values causes many people to live in their minds or to induce altered states. Much of what you most deeply value and long to experience is difficult to find anywhere else at this time.

It may be apparent to you that planet Earth is in chaos. Do not let that threaten you. If you are prepared to actualize inspiration, whatever you need will become available when you need it. When comprehension of the state you call "chaos" was needed, there arose a discipline of *chaos theory* and the theorists to study it. Those on your planet who are developing this field have realized that chaos is not aberrant; chaos is part of the integrity of nature.

All processes of life on Earth are either processes of realization or processes of transformation. In any transformative process there is chaos. Chaos is a natural state of energy that has been liberated from a collective or subjective pattern and is not yet refocused with integrity. Chaos is also a state produced and inhabited by Beings who have made accommodations they are unable to maintain. Their inability to continue to conform to these self-limitations produces chaos within their own energy constellation. It also produces chaos within the environments they supported during their self-limiting accommodations.

The key to more graceful chaos in your process of societal transformation is to promote and support a reprioritization of values. This challenge calls for you to shift your focus from "having" to "being." This will not put an end to enterprise and acquisition. It will insure their integrity and social responsibility. You are called to redesign the existing structures of your society to higher levels of function. It will serve you to recognize your visionaries and allow them to collectively guide you in this. Existing structures need to be preserved. The continuity of structure prevents disorientation. When new functions become integral, necessary transformations of structure are evident to all and readily undertaken. To imagine that you will do everything in a different way is to assure escalating personal and social chaos. To imagine that you will do many things the same way but with greater understanding and integrity is to produce a stable ground for transformation.

How will these changes come about when economic momentum seems to circumscribe public dialogue, creativity and social consciousness? It appears to most of you that this governor is so imbedded in your planetary systems it has unstoppable momentum. Economic momentum is not unstoppable; it is just circular. To open the circle and free its energy you need only align with higher values —*being* instead of *having*; *aligning* instead of *competing*; *supporting* instead of *controlling*. With the participation and support of your transformational population, these changes will open the economic circle. Highly functional systems of barter will be among the first indicators of social cohesion beyond the existing economic model. When you redefine the goods and services you need and develop integrous means for providing them to yourselves, you will have invented a social healing medium that can be Universally supported. Then the economic circle will transform.

Change and progress occur when some of you who have been maintaining circular behavior elevate your course. In coming to a well known juncture on your journey around the circle, you recognize that continuing on such a course would mean perpetual repetition. In that moment you make a higher choice than you have previously made, freeing yourself from circular repetitions. When any person does this, their circle is broken. It becomes a spiral. While many people continue to repeat their limiting circles in protection of their status quo, transformation of a society is dependent upon those who have the strength and courage to break from the circle and produce spirals to higher levels of choice and expression…and higher …and higher. Eventually these spirals connect each dimension of reality to the next. A self-realized person lives in an endless "slinky" of Universal access and integral experience.

To grow is to progress in your understanding of values. Each circle and spiral expresses the consciousness of those who value it. Each circle and spiral of consciousness is the "truth" to those who value it. People populate a circle because their respective values require them to sickle a pathway through

that specific unenlightened ground of being—to bring that
ground to enlightenment in themselves and the collective.
Even though many people become entrenched in their circular
positions, losing touch with their Soul purpose for being
there, they are nonetheless inhabiting their circles to mean-
ingfully serve themselves and Humanity.

———————————— ✒✒ ————————————

There are circles and spirals expressing every imaginable value.
People holding on to the *old* and people aspiring to the *new* sit
next to one another on every bus, in every restaurant, across every
national and philosophical border. The old of one value and the
new of another live in the same individual. Is that person part of
the old or the new? What is old to one person is new to another.
This needs to be remembered and respected. Life can encompass
all these relative realities. It always has.

What is currently changing in the world is the expansiveness of
Human consciousness and the understanding of what it means to
be a person. Supported by changes in planetary frequency amplitude and magnetism, a growing number of people are becoming
aware of their multidimensional nature and of essential Universal
values. So many of you are expanding your consciousness that the
disparity between societal values and essential values is demanding
to be reconciled. That is why this is such a difficult, creative and
transformative time for all of you.

Transformation does not occur by replacing one limited circle with
another. Any circle that goes around and around without elevating
to a higher expression, turns quickly into a limited system and a
potential entrapment. Have you not found that there is always

more to learn, that every understanding you come to is eventually replaced by a yet higher understanding of the same thing? Some call it maturing, some call it aging and some call it expanding consciousness. Call it what you will, every Being in the Universe experiences this. In spite of this commonly shared experience, some people and ideological constituencies assert fixed answers to expanding questions, insisting upon locating in three dimensions the multidimensional nature of life. If you have experienced the challenges of surrendering control to an inner-directed life, it is easy to understand why these people find comfort and stability in placing reality within intellectual or spiritual controls. Due to innocence, or to ignorance such as misaligned devotion, these people are limiting their potentials in order to preserve their immediate purposes and beliefs.

It is understandable that children who were conscripted to conform to the academic, religious and conceptual systems of unenlightened predecessors have conceived the value and meaning of their lives in relation to these systems and are invested in perpetuating them. As shortsighted as this may seem to those who have spiraled further, this behavior is consistent with their circle of awareness. As such, it deserves respect throughout the Universe.

The spirit that moves the New Age seeker is the same spirit that moves the fundamentalist. Although they may appear to be polarities, both are moved by devotion and by their desire to realize union with their Source. Both are seeking to live their lives in a way they believe aligns them with their God.

Some people go around the same circle for years, working at a job from which they derive no pleasure and to which they contribute little of their essential value. Some people break their circle to spiral up, redefining their security to be that which secures their full-heartedness and their integrity. Such a leap is no small thing in a society where Beings are dependent upon one another's approval rather than upon one another's understanding and love, in order to succeed and attain material comfort. Many people try to leap, but finding no immediate place to land lose trust in their instincts and inspirations. Those who *do* leap, and manage to flap their wings long enough to discover where they have arrived, will always find new ground to stand on. These individuals are explorers. They liberate the system and elevate the collective ground of being. Without necessarily knowing what comes next, they know they must leap in order to live in a way that maintains their integrity.

Not knowing what comes next is scary for many people. To secure themselves they want to produce an ideology and a projected description for the next level before they get there. When the explorers who are leaping for new ground presume to describe destinations at which they have not yet arrived, inappropriate dogmas and ideologies are formulated that eventually collapse and define new circles of limitation.

What is currently being called the New Age movement is at risk of defining itself into such a circle of limitation. In the name of higher consciousness, competitive materialism can be reconceived and disguised in another dress. One need only recognize the problems of the competitive majority duplicated in the economics of the New Age movement, to see that the New Age spiral could easily collapse into another circle of self-limitation. The New Age movement, like any pathway, can produce open-ended spirals only if it transcends manipulation and competition, defines its purposes and not its ends, and focuses itself in integrity, simplicity and service.

To attune to the vastness of nature, to construct spirals instead of circles and to learn to leap, Humanity needs new understanding and new ways of seeing. It is time for you to integrate the knowledge offered in these letters and in numerous other writings and teachings currently available in the world. This knowledge does not polarize with religion or science. It is knowledge of the multidimensional nature of things, inclusive of religion and science. It is a practical and spirit-endowed wisdom.

Humanity conceived of quantum leaps in order to prepare itself to make them. When it does—when leaping becomes a preferred alternative to walking the linear path or repeating the circle—Humankind will be one leap from flying. This process is important to the whole of the Universe. The rhythms of consciousness that unify all states of being and give a Being in any one system of reality access to all others, live within the leap.

The art of leaping needs to be taught. Education, physics, sociology, psychology, spirituality, anthropology and medicine are among the systems of knowledge ready for renovation. They are stretching to make their circles big enough to contain their expanding awareness, but they must spiral. They must leap...and they must teach leaping.

Never has there been a time on Earth when the pull on static circles and the spread of spirals has been so great. The huge slinky of consciousness is extending itself. Each circle and spiral is dependent upon the integrity of the whole. There will come a point of critical momentum. When enough spirals have the momentum to pull the remaining closed circles, the whole slinky will move to a new position. You are poised on the threshold of this transformative momentum. Its fulfillment will be transmutation.

Those people who inhabit circles that are pulled along by the spiraling momentum of others may have no awareness of where they are, where they were, or even that they have moved. They may reproduce the same circle relative to an expanded context and live within it as before, not noticing any change at all. This is how a reality system progresses through transmutation without imposing its rhythms on those who make choices that restrain them from participation. In this way the integrity of each individual is equally respected and responded to by the nature of the system.

The question that cannot be answered is: Will the transformational population have sufficient impact to magnetize all of Humanity into planetary transmutation; or, will they expand their consciousness and the dimensionality of Earth, creating an adjunct reality context for those who are ready to progress into Universal consciousness?

No one can presume to know another's course of self-invention. The butterfly created itself as a caterpillar to express the unlimited nature of transmutation. Ideally, not one among you would be robbed of the magic and challenge of timely discovery. Each of you is in your right time. Each of you is doing the best you can—not the best you can think about or imagine, but the best you can actually do, given your personal variables of consciousness and your realization of love. No one has to be rushed for your world to progress. Those who need to be tugged a little will put themselves in positions to be tugged. Those who need to innovate will innovate. Those who need to hold to familiar ground to nourish their self confidence or creativity will hold firm—and eventually transform that ground for others. The contributions of those who appear to be slowest will not be needed until they are ready to make them.

When you do not see the way, it may be inventing itself before you. Trust the nature of things. Permit the nature of things. You are not called upon to rely on blind faith. Let your faith spring from what you have actually seen and felt; from what rings you like a bell of truth, making goose bumps on your arms; and from the transformation that is becoming apparent. You do not need to fix the world; it is not broken! Like a heart that *feels* broken, it is in the throes of transformation. Its pieces will fall into depths unknown. From that place of discovery it will regenerate with resilience and compassion, able to access heights unknown. You need only sustain a supportive and trusting environment to nurture this transformation of your life and all life. It is important to the whole of the Universe that each of you come into greater love and understanding.

This is the challenge of an Age of Inspired Realism. 𝒥

YOUR NAME - PLEASE PRINT CLEARLY

ADDRESS

CITY, STATE, ZIP

MAIL TO:

Inspired Company
P.O. Box 10
Mill Valley, CA 94942

If you choose to sign here, your signature gives us your permission to print or quote the contents of your letter.

You may detach this letter paper at the performance and use it to write back to us, or you may make copies of this page. We regret that we cannot return anything you send to us.

We invite you to ask questions or share a Universal experience.

YOUR NAME - PLEASE PRINT CLEARLY

ADDRESS

CITY, STATE, ZIP

MAIL TO:

Inspired Company
P.O. Box 10
Mill Valley, CA 94942

If you choose to sign here, your signature gives us your permission to print or quote the contents of your letter.

This is a permanent page in your book. You may copy this page of letter paper and use it to write back to us. We regret that we cannot return anything you send to us.

We invite you to ask questions or share a Universal experience.